Lisa,
You ca
do anything 'y
want to when you
believe in yourself!
Dare 2 Dream!

Catherine
Weands
5.14.81

# POSITIVE POWER PEOPLE

*This book is dedicated to
our business Associate, Laura Webb.
Her sunny smile, constant support, and
dedication to the work have made
the publishing of this volume a pleasure.
From all of the authors, and the publisher,
our thanks to Laura.*

# POSITIVE POWER PEOPLE

*The Enlightenment Amplifiers*

Royal CBS Publishing, Glendora, California 91740

ROYAL CASSETTES • BOOKS • SPEECHES
ROYAL CBS PUBLISHING

Positive Power People

Royal CBS Publishing
600 West Foothill Blvd.
Glendora, California 91740

First Edition

Library of Congress Cataloging in Publication Date in Progress

ISBN 0-934344-07-8

Printed in the United States of America

Design and Production: BC Graphics, Glendora, CA

"The Enlightenment Amplifiers"

*By Dottie Walters, C.S.P.*

*Rosetta Stone turn 'round and 'round...*
*Unlock your secret mark!*
*Hyroglyphics lost from us*
*In Egypt's cryptic dark.*

Sun with rays "RA"

Star, to teach

*Seekers turned the Stone once more...*
*Out fell the first word, "RA!"*
*Their word for God, Their word for sun,*
*"Enlightenment!"...We saw!*

Giraffe, to foretell

Dance, joy, jubilate

Arms extended
Be ignorant of,
do not know

*Deciphered soon were many more*
*"Giraffe" meant, "look ahead!"*
*"Jubilation!" was a dance...*
*"Hands up, - Who knows?", they said.*

Ankh - Life
Mirrors
made in
this shape,
as a pun

*And then we found the word called "Ankh!"*
*Formed in a mirror's shape*
*"Ra hands us life, don't miss the point.*
*God's gift, for us to take!"*

Eye - to see
understand

*A pun that's lived five thousand years*
*"Look deep, here secrets lie,*
*What does a mirror mean, but life?"*
*Old Pharaoh winks his eye.*

*vi*

## CAVETT ROBERT
*President Emeritus National*
*Speakers Association*

Cavett Robert is the recipient of the coveted Golden Gavel Award from Toastmasters International, was named "America's Professional Salesman" by the National Association of Realtors, and in 1973 was elected one of the two "Speakers of the Year" after a canvass of over 10,000 program chairmen, meeting planners, executive directors and corporations.

Freedom Foundation of Valley Forge chose Cavett Robert as recipient of an award for patriotism through his speeches and writings. The presentation was made at an award dinner by Senator Barry Goldwater.

# *Foreword*

## *By Cavett Robert*

From time immemorial the world has seen two kinds of power. PEOPLE POWER and that imaginative, vague, insecure power which people feel a certain important position can give them.

This great book is devoted to the first concept of power - the only one on which any permanent success can be based.

There is perhaps no one in America who is doing more to help other people develop this POSITIVE POWER within themselves than Dottie Walters. Her whole philosophy of life as expressed in her numerous speeches and writings is that if a person has a sincere and passionate desire to accomplish anything in life, that divine ambition has within itself the power to create all the necessary ingredients for success. This great divine creative quality has been given the name by Dottie of POSITIVE PEOPLE POWER.

Dottie has brought together a great group of wonderful people and inspired them to share the best of their life's experiences and philosophies with others.

It is my personal feeling that no one individual can write a book which offers as much as a number of successful individuals can offer by sharing the very best of themselves. If there is a spark of divinity or fragment of eternity on this earth it is found in this divine sharing which has permeated every project of any kind sponsored by Dottie Walters.

Please keep in mind two things when you are reading this book:

First, no individual could live long enough to learn through experience the great lessons of life contained in this fabulous book. Please eat, digest and assimilate its precious contents carefully.

Second, you will note throughout this book that goals and experiences, in the mind of the writer are not as important as what they become in seeking these goals. This is a great principle of life, often neglected, but emphasized throughout the chapters of this book.

And what is it that is developed in their Pilgrim's journey in search of the "pot of gold at the end of the rainbow?" It is found in the title to this book - POSITIVE PEOPLE POWER.

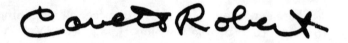

"If you have anything really valuable to contribute to the world it will come through the expression of your own personality - that single spark of divinity that sets you off and makes you different from every other living creature."

Bruce Barton of: Barton, Batten, Dustin
and Osburn Advertising

"*Dare to be wise: BEGIN! One who postpones the hour of living rightly is like the rustic who waits for the river to run out before he crosses, - yet on it glides, and will glide on forever.*"

*Horace*

Dottie Walters receives CSP (Certified Speaking Professional) Certification, at National Speakers Association Convention. She was one of the first four women in the United States to be so designated. Making the presentation is Ty Boyd, President of National Speakers Association.

Dottie Walters
Author, President of four corporations, Booking Agent, Seminar Leader, Publisher, Advertising Executive
Royal CBS
600 W. Foothill Blvd.
Glendora, CA 91740
(213) 335-0218

## DOTTIE WALTERS, C.S.P.

Dottie began her advertising business by pushing her two small children before her on a baby stroller. Pulling from the inspiration of her high school English teacher who had insisted she take journalism, Dottie trod dusty roads in her rural community to find the Baldwin Park Bulletin office. "There are no jobs!" she was told. But at that moment she turned her life around. "Then *sell* me *Ad* space!" she pleaded. After the newspaper staff agreed, she asked for the first week's space on credit. Then began the long journey, selling advertisements to the local merchants. Grasping *Every Idea* she could see, Dottie educated herself by reading biographies, six or seven each week. She haunted the library, and attended every seminar in her area.

The advertising business grew. She was asked to speak for service clubs. Today her advertising business spans five counties, with four offices. Four thousand merchants use the services of Hospitality Hostess, a welcoming company. Dottie has spoken across the United States, Canada and England. She has been featured on national television, radio, and in numerous newspapers.

She is author of the famous NEVER UNDER-ESTIMATE THE SELLING POWER OF A WOMAN, Publisher of SUCCESS SECRETS, and THE PEARL OF POTENTIALITY, plus HERE IS GENIUS, and now POSITIVE POWER PEOPLE.

Dottie has numerous fine Cassette programs on the market, and is a happy wife, mother and grandmother. Dottie Walters is publisher of a newsletter for speakers, "Sharing Ideas," is active in the National Speakers Association, and is featured in Who's Who in American Woman and many other similar publications. Dottie is famous for her Inspiration, Practical Philosophy and "CAN DO" Spirit. Her friends say "She inspires us."

## POSITIVE POWER PEOPLE

"The Enlightenment Amplifiers"

# INTRODUCTION

*By Dottie Walters*

*"Books which teach and speak of whatever is highest and best are equally sacred, whatever be the tongue in which they are written, or the nation to which they belong."*

*Benedict de Spinoza*

These statements, all alike, although made many years apart, flow into a pulsing beam of enlightenment. *"Let there be light,"* God says in Genesis 1:3, *"And there was light."* High school drop-out Albert Einstein was told he would never amount to anything by his teachers. But when he read Bernstein's PEOPLES BOOK OF NATURAL SCIENCE, the very first page electrified his mind. Al wondered, (that beautiful state of mind) *"What would the world look like if we could travel on a beam of light? - To travel on a beam of light! - One Hundred and Eighty-Six Thousand miles per second."* Einstein later discovered every atom of our bodies is made up of this fabulous light energy, 186,000 MPS-SQUARED!

Einstein later said, *"Enlightenment, - genius, - is a flashflood. Associating with people of Genius sparks the mind like a striking flint. We must deal with people who let ideas flow through them. We must listen to them. We must associate with people who solve problems. You will recognize these people because they create, combine, change, amplify and animate. They ignore the skeptics of the worlds who sit back and criticize. "*

What a fascinating quotation when you understand the acronym for LASER *"Light Amplification by Stimulated Emission of Radiation. "*

The third statement was made on July 7, 1960 by Dr. Theodore H. Maiman, when he announced:

*"Mankind has succeeded in achieving a goal that scientists have sought for many years. 'Coherent light' has been attained. The long-sought 'laser' is no longer an elusive dream. "*

A variety of substances can be used to produce laser beams. One of the most commonly used is extremely pure ruby crystal. Each end of a ruby rod is coated with a reflecting surface. Then the rod is energized by a source of intense light. Atoms in the ruby crystal absorb this energy and emit photons, the basic unit of light energy. These photons bounce back and forth between the two mirrored ends of the ruby rod, and more and more photons are added until the light energy becomes so intense that a beam of laser light finally passes right through one of the rod's mirrored ends.

The difference between this light beam and the beam produced by a flashlight is what makes the laser such an important scientific breakthrough. The light waves produced by the glowing filament in ordinary light bulbs are emitted in a broad range of wavelengths and in every direction. In a laser beam, the light waves are all of the same wavelength and are parallel, like a battalion of well-drilled soldiers marching in lockstep. This is why laser light is called "coherent" and is many times more intense than ordinary light.

Once the laser light emerges it can be sharply focused on an area as small as a few ten millionths of an inch in diameter (the head of an ordinary straight pin is almost 2 million times larger).

What happens when human beings focus their enlightenment? In 1919 Harry Emerson Fosdick said,

*"No stream or gas ever drives anything until it is confined. No Niagara is ever turned into light and power until it is channeled. No human life ever grows until it is focused, dedicated, disciplined,"*

Thus focusing the power of your mind, concentrating, is the key to becoming a POSITIVE POWER PERSON. Light is universal, and available to all humans. It is a fact unquestioned. Four thousand years ago the Pharoah Akhnaton, who built his temples to the one God, "Ra" prayed,

*"Lordly thou climbest the heavenly mountain of light, eternal sun, origin of life..Thou has created the world after thy liking. Thou gavest sustenance to all living creatures forever. Thou apportionest to each his span of life. Thou are the pounding of my heart. All that we perceive in thy light shall perish, but thou shalt live and prosper for ever more."*

And our Bible told us nearly 2,000 years ago, *"Ye are all the Children of light and the children of the day."* I Thess.

Our brains themselves are small electrical generators, causing billions of electrical impulses to flash every second through the endless pathways of our minds. As knowledge enters our minds our cells or neurons constantly chatter to each other in an ebb and flow of thoughts. In 1820, Thomas Carlyle said, *"Be careful what you think about, for you will surely get it."*

Scientist Thomas Lewis explained in 1980 that *Ideas, called 'notions', are actual, and are shaped with prongs. When they enter the mind they search for similar 'notions'. When they find the same 'prongs', the notions dock. When enough thoughts have docked, they form an aggregate. When there is a large enough aggregate, the person acts!*

In 1950, Albert Sweitzer, the great doctor humanitarian summed it up this way:

*"The power of ideas is incalculable. We see no power in a drop of water. But let it get into a crack in the rock and be turned to ice, and it splits the rock; turned into steam, it drives the pistons of the most powerful engines. Something has happened to it which makes active and effective power that is latent in it.*

*So it is with ideas. Ideas are thoughts. So long as they exist merely as thoughts, the power latent in them remains ineffective, however great the enthusiasm, and however strong the conviction with which the thought is held. Their power becomes effective only when they are taken up into human personality, and acted on."*

Therefore it is vital that we let enlightenment into our minds. This book contains the stories of the most positive people! The kind Einstein suggested we must associate with. Let their positive enlightenment flow from these pages into the neurons of your mind.

You are the ruby! Your ideas will bounce back and forth, amplifying these ideas. Your creative expressiveness will burst forth, like the beam of a laser to focus on great new possibilities in your life. Open the channel! Turn on the switch! The Positive Power awaits your touch!

# the pharaoh's secret

by DOTTIE WALTERS

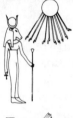

The ancient Egyptians wrote the secret of achievement, of leadership, in the largest, most mysterious symbol mankind has ever constructed. It has lain on the sands for centuries for those who have the eye to read its cryptic message.

What is the secret of the leader? Just watch an orchestra performing, or a group rowing a shell. What does the conductor, the coxswain, have? The beat. No one ever follows a limp leader. No, the leader's ear is the one that hears an energy beat. It begins with this person's own pulse. It is repeated in the movement of the sun and stars in this solar system, again in the rhythmic tempo of the universe, and back again in the atom itself. This is the believing ear of Management. A Cynic states "seeing is believing," the Dreamer-Doer-Manager knows believing must be done before actuality can be accomplished.

Shakespeare heard the planets' rhythm. "Listen to the music of the Spheres," he tells us. In 1643 Thomas Brown caught their melody when he wrote, "There is music whenever there is harmony, order and proportion. It is the music of the Spheres."

The energy tempo is the banging, clanging industry of the job being conceived, completed and delivered. The production of the world.

How fascinating that when the atom was smashed, the scientists discovered what God already knew. At the center remained a pulsing beat.

Paracelsus of Switzerland called the beat Quintessence. Life Energy. Put your fingers to your pulse, and feel it. Visualize the 5 (quin) points of the pyramid of the Egyptians. The top is the Nucleus, while the four corners are the protors and electrons singing around it in their ringing patterns. The atom in stone!

Doers like Milton, the blind poet heard it. "Ring out ye crystal spheres, move in melodious time!" From the universe to the atom, to ourselves, there is a beat in everything. Ralph Waldo Emerson tells us,

"·hear a sky born music still
'tis not in high stars alone
But in the mud and scum of things,-
Alway, alway, something sings!"

Listen. . .Listen! If you hear it, know now: We carry within us the wonders we seek without. Arise and go. You know the Pharaoh's Secret. You are the one to get the job done.

"The Enlightenment Amplifiers"

*"To be rich in admiration and free from envy; to rejoice greatly in the good of others; to love with such generosity of heart that your love is still a dear possession in absence or unkindness - these are the gifts of fortune which money cannot buy and with which money can buy nothing. He who has such a treasury of riches, being happy and valiant himself, in his own nature, will enjoy the universe as if it were his own estate, and help the man to whom he lends a hand to enjoy it with him.*

*Robert Louis Stevenson*

# POSITIVE
# POWER
# PEOPLE

**BILLY BURDEN**
4404 S. Florida Avenue, Suite 12
Lakeland, Florida 33803
(813) 644-4888

## BILLY BURDEN

Dynamic   *   Inspirational   *   Challenging
Entertaining   *   Dedicated

Each of these words is needed to describe Billy Burden. A man of many talents and interests, Billy Burden is often called the "Poet for the People." He is an unexcelled champion of man's right to be successful at anything he wants to accomplish.

Recognized as America's foremost memory training expert, he is the founder of the Billy Burden School of Memory and Attitude. His MEMORY MASTER® method demonstrates that a positive memory gets positive results. His students include employees of such companies as General Motors, General Electric, AT & T, Westinghouse, IBM, Sears, Honeywell, Johns-Mansville, and numerous other Fortune Five Hundred Companies.

His most recent book, "WHEN THE GOING GETS TOUGH," is, according to Dr. Norman Vincent Peale, a book that will give you fresh courage, wise insights, and a restored faith in your own ability to overcome any problem.

He is one of America's most popular speakers, and at various rallies across the country he shares the stage regularly with such greats as Paul Harvey, Art Linkletter, Earl Nightingale, Dr. Robert Schuller, and others. He is a member of the National Speakers Association, International Platform Association, and the American Society of Training and Development. It is estimated that he has spoken personally to over a million people in the past eighteen months.

His timely recording of "Something Ought To Be Said" and "This Is My Flag" is getting tremendous response from radio listeners all across America.

**POSITIVE POWER PEOPLE**

*The Enlightenment Amplifiers*

# POSITIVE IS FORWARD

### By Billy Burden

*"One of the most important things to get across to the modern world is an understanding of the power of prayer. Prayer is thought contact with the Holy Spirit. It is the greatest power in the world!*
### Cecil B. DeMille

When Dottie Walters, president of Royal CBS Publishing Company, asked me to write the first chapter for POSITIVE POWER PEOPLE, I was humbly honored. And I was doubly honored when I found out that my warm and wonderful friend, Cavett Robert, President Emeritus of National Speakers Association, had been asked to write the foreword for this book.

You see, Cavett exemplifies POSITIVE POWER PEOPLE in action. I have had the privilege of appearing with him on many, many programs from coast to coast, and he is truly, at age 73, a giant of a man. He is constantly giving of himself in order that others might become POSITIVE POWER PEOPLE. As one of my mentors, he has, time and time again, given me, and countless others, encouragement when it was needed, and he stands as a constant source of inspiration.

Yes, Dottie and Cavett, I am honored to write the first chapter for this book.

Every good writer feels a responsibility to his readers to give them something that will leave them a little richer for having taken the time to read what he has written.

Some writers write to entertain. If this is the writer's purpose and if the reader is entertained, then the writer fulfills his obligation to the reader. If the writer's purpose is to give the reader inspiration and if the reader is inspired from reading the writer's words, the writer's obligation is again fulfilled. If the purpose of the writing is to inform and instruct the reader on "how to" do this or that and if the reader finds the answers, then, again, the writer fulfills his obligation to the reader.

I find that I always feel a strong sense of obligation to my readers when I begin to write. This chapter is certainly no exception. In fact, with a great mentor "up front," I feel an obligation stronger than ever to the readers of this book as I write this first chapter.

In thinking, introspectively, before starting to write this chapter, I asked myself, "What is it that the reader will expect to get from this book? Will he expect to learn the value of being a positive person? Will he hope to find inspiration and encouragement as he reads about the lives of positive people? Will he be searching for ways that he can become positive? Will he be looking for ways to stay positive once he gets that way?"

As I asked myself what I would expect from reading this book, I realized that I would expect all of these.

In my book WHEN THE GOING GETS TOUGH , published by the Fleming H. Revell Company, I started the book by saying, "When the going gets tough, the tough get going. Great! And most of us have heard that cliche before. But the more important question is - how do the tough get tough when the going gets that way?"

Burden/6

Then I proceeded to boil the answer down to eight little words. So it is with this book.

*How To Be Positive*

Many readers will already know the positive power that belongs to positive people, but many of these same readers will not know how to be positive when everything around them seems to turn up negative and things keep crashing in on their lives.

It doesn't happen by accident. It certainly is not an innate ability with which some are born. It isn't inherited. One cannot buy it.

Well, then, where does one get this POSITIVE POWER?

You will be happy to know that it is a learned attribute and it is available to everyone. It is not possessed solely by the affluent. Wealth does not guarantee it. The most common peasant can possess this POSITIVE POWER and thereby be one of the happiest people on the face of the earth.

You say, "I'm interested. Tell me more!"

Okay, you're on!

Do with the doers!

Move with the movers and win with the winners!

People possessing POSITIVE POWER are DOERS! They are MOVERS, and they are WINNERS!

Let's take a look, for a moment, at the value of being a positive person.

First of all, if you can do as the song says and eliminate the negative in your life and accentuate the positive, you'll simply have more "bounce" in your step. And when you have more bounce in your step, you'll be able to step over obstacles along the way.

You'll have enthusiasm. Your system will be able to give you that added shot of epinephrine in your blood stream when you need an extra surge of power for the job at hand.

When you possess this POSITIVE POWER, you'll be able to dream dreams worth dreaming. You'll be able to build dreams that can build you.

*Finding Hope*

With this POSITIVE POWER, you'll be able to find hope in the face of adversity. You'll be able to see a ray of sunshine through a break in the clouds. You'll be able to believe in "someday," and you'll be able to turn your somedays into today.

Not bad! Wouldn't you say?

But what about the other side of the coin?

Just for a moment, let's remove the positive and examine the negative.

Without the power that comes with being positive, you will often find yourself paralyzed and unable to move ahead.

Without this POSITIVE POWER, your sky will become a blanket of dark clouds which the sun cannot penetrate.

Any dreams you might have will burst like bubbles in your face.

Gloom will set in and, eventually, you will join the ranks of eighty percent of the people who, according to the American Medical Association, have illnesses which are psychosomatic in origin.

Eventually, as surely as you are reading this sentence, without this POSITIVE POWER, you will find yourself sinking into the mire of mediocrity and self pity; and the lower you sink, the harder it is to surface again.

Well, the picture is rather obvious, isn't it? The rewards that come with being positive are many. The despair that comes without it can bring ruin.

I can personally attest to this. My life has not always been filled with the positive.

It is not hard for me to remember a rather poverty stricken childhood. I remember the day the neighbors brought a basket of food to our house so that we'd have something to eat. I remember the day we were so hungry my mother had to kill my only pet, a little Bantam hen, and cook it so that we would have something to eat. Dad was out of town working, and mother was penniless. But hungry as I was, I could not eat a single bit of my little Bantam hen.

This type of experience can be very traumatic and can have a negative effect on one's life. In fact, it can be devastating.

When, as a child, you wear clothes with patches on top of patches, you begin to develop a shy, introverted personality. You begin to walk with your head down instead of holding it high like those around you.

Of course, while these things are happening, without your realizing it, your being is busy nurturing tough fibers. And then, later on, when you discover the power that comes with being positive, you have a strong fabric to go with it.

While this fabric is forming, you are learning to have compassion and feeling for others.

## What Is Character?

Your personality may need some polish here and there, but your character is well established. And this isn't really too bad, because personality is what you are when others are looking. But, as Dwight L. Moody said, "Character is what you are in the dark."

I thank God for my character, which was molded from the clay of poverty.

Too, I thank God that somewhere along the way I was able to burst out of my cocoon of negativism and dress myself in a suit tailored from a positive fabric.

Certainly, I am thankful that, like most people who

have been able to find this positive fabric, I have a desire, each day of my life, to help others find the power that comes with being positive.

For many years, and from coast to coast, I have been conducting memory seminars helping people from all walks of life to remember with ease. I never teach one of my memory seminars without touching on the value of a positive mental attitude.

In my opinion, they go hand in glove. I have had literally thousands of men and women say, "Billy, I want to thank you for my better memory, and I also want to thank you for a more positive attitude."

Some reading this might wonder how a better memory can give one a positive attitude and, in turn, POSITIVE POWER.

When you stop to analyze the following points, I think the reasons will be rather obvious.

*Memory Power*

When you are able, for instance, to remember names and faces and when you can call a person by his name, your stock with that person goes up in value. You're able to possess self-confidence, and this self-confidence allows you to cultivate positive thoughts.

When you are able to remember what you read, you are able to be better informed, and you are able to draw from your reservoir of wisdom. Automatically, with this ability comes POSITIVE POWER.

A student who was on the verge of failing yesterday but is at the top of his class today, thanks to his ability to remember with ease, cannot help becoming more positive.

The benefits go on and on.

When you fill your mind with positive thoughts there will be no room for the negatives.

Try to fill a barrel with water and air at the same time. Impossible! One must go. As the water is put in, the air goes out, or vice versa. You cannot have a barrel full of water and a barrel full of air at the same time. So it is with your mind. Fill it with positive thoughts and there will be no room for negative thoughts.

Now, if you've never been positive, you may be saying, "Sounds good, but how do I become positive?"

Well, do you want to be conventional or unconventional? Both ways work.

Have you ever applied for a job in a suit that went out of style five years earlier because you didn't have the current year's version? It's hard to be positive during a job interview when you know you are not properly dressed.

I recall a time in my life when I sold life insurance. The things I learned from the man who trained me helped me to start pulling the positive strings in my life.

Some might have said that he was "nuts," and, at times, there were days I knew that he was, but even then I could see with my own eyes the results he was getting.

I remember days when he took me "out in the field" for training. Even though our appointment with the prospect might not be until 11:00 A.M., we would leave the office around 9:30 A.M. and we would head straight for the drug store, where he would buy a cigar. Not just any cigar but the most expensive one they had in the store. As I recall, even back then, the best one sold for around a dollar.

He would light that thing up and we would head straight for the barber shop, where he would get two things even if he didn't need them. While he puffed away on that cigar, he would get a hair trim and a shoe shine.

There were times when I was certain that he was stark raving mad. I have sat and watched the barber make the scissors go "click-click" on his neck, but the poor man could not cut off any more hair because he had cut it all off the day before.

*Feel Like A Million*

Want to know what happened next? When we left that barber shop, the man training me felt like a "million dollars," and he had POSITIVE POWER.

Have you ever known a lady who didn't feel great as she left the beauty shop? Of course not.

So it was with the man training me. The trip to the barber shop made him feel great. What's more - the prospect never had a prayer. I never once saw this man fail to turn an interview into a sale.

Unorthodox? Certainly! But the proof of the pudding is in the eating. His commissions often amounted to several hundred dollars. What was five or even ten dollars for a shoe shine, a hair trim, and the best cigar in town?

Thankfully, there are more conventional ways to have this POSITIVE POWER. One is free for the taking.

Read the Bible.

It is a perpetual source for an abundant harvest of positive thoughts.

The book of Proverbs is filled with thoughts for POSITIVE POWER.

I suppose that, more than any other scriptures, two have allowed me to become positive when nothing else could help.

*If You Have Faith*

First, Matthew 17:20 "...If ye have faith as a grain of mustard seed, ye shall say unto this mountain, Remove hence to yonder place; and it shall remove; and nothing shall be impossible unto you."

And Matthew 7:7 "Ask, and it shall be given you; seek, and ye shall find; knock, and it shall be opened unto you:"

In addition to the Bible, there are hundreds of good books on the market filled with inspiration and ideas that can be the spark to ignite POSITIVE POWER within you.

Since Dr. Norman Vincent Peale wrote THE POWER OF POSITIVE THINKING, thousands of men and women have found POSITIVE POWER by reading it. But what I think is even more wonderful is that many of these same men and women have gone on to write books of their own on the subject and they have, in turn, helped thousands more find this same POSITIVE POWER.

*Listening To Learn*

In my opinion, one of the most valuable learning tools ever devised is the cassette tape. There are many great cassette programs available that are invaluable to those seeking POSITIVE POWER.

Most people in America today spend considerable time in their automobiles. For some, this time is simply lost. For others, however, this time is some of the most productive time in their day.

They learn and find POSITIVE POWER by listening to cassette tapes.

I have countless letters from men and women all over the country who write to let me know that by listening to my MEMORY MASTER® memory tapes, while they are driving to and from work, they have found the secrets for being able to remember with ease.

Many men listen to tapes while they are shaving. Many women listen while they are applying their make-up. Many families learn together as they listen to tapes as a family project.

Now, how do you stay positive once you get that way? The same way you got positive in the first place! You keep on getting more positive.

Remember, when you stop getting better, you stop being good. You cannot stand still. Either you are moving forward or you are slipping backward.

*Positive is forward.*
*Negative is backward.*
*When growth stops, decay sets in.*

I know that you will marvel at the POSITIVE POWER possessed by the people who share their lives and ideas with you in the chapters which follow.

I promise you a bumper crop and a rewarding harvest from the positive seeds you plant and cultivate in your life each day.

"...for whatsoever a man soweth, that shall he also reap."

Galatians 6:7

### "I KNOW I CAN"

*I played with life like a game,*
*To find that Life would do the same.*
*I wondered why at the end of each day,*
*Nothing worthwhile had come my way.*

*Then I decided to make myself a plan,*
*And I told myself, "I KNOW I CAN."*
*Sure enough, it happened on that day,*
*Everything started to come my way.*

*You too can do just like me,*
*For that matter, so can anybody.*
*Get yourself a plan,*
*And tell yourself, "I KNOW I CAN."*

[*Poem Copyright 1962 by Billy Burden*]

NOTE: If you would like a brochure about Billy Burden's MEMORY MASTER® memory course or a free copy of "I KNOW I CAN," printed on 8 x 10 parchtex for framing, you may write him at P.O. Box 5500, Lakeland, Florida 33803.

**LilyB MOSKAL**
Island Club, 101 Orchid Bldg.
777 S. Federal Hwy.
Pompano Beach, Florida 33062

## LilyB MOSKAL

LilyB Moskal, known as "The Gal With the Million Dollar Attitude", is a nationally known speaker, author, sales/management trainer and consultant who has had successful careers as a TV broadcaster, teacher, realtor, professional speaker as well as a wife, mother of four and recently, a grandmother! She travels extensively speaking, training and motivating others to achieve their potential, to learn how to develop self esteem in order to become more successful AND happier!

LilyB (and that really IS her entire first name!) and her husband, Tom, maintain offices as well as residences in both Pompano Beach, Florida and Washington D.C. area. She received a B.A. degree in Speech Communications by working her way through the University of Southwestern Louisiana and was awarded a scholarship for graduate study in education at Tulane University. However, she claims that her proudest credential is - experience! LilyB tells it like it is - from experience with enthusiasm coupled with humor.

Active in the National Association of REALTORS, LilyB served on the Board of Directors of the National Speakers Association and as charter president of the Florida Chapter. She is an instructor on the faculties of the Graduate REALTORS Institute, is listed in WHO'S WHO OF AMERICAN WOMEN, PERSONALITIES OF THE SOUTH, NATIONAL DIRECTORY OF SPEAKERS, and has contributed numerous articles to professional publications. As a TV Broadcaster she hosted her own, daily "talk" program over WWOM-TV in New Orleans, her home-town, and was chosen as Woman of the Year in 1970. The Honor Society of Phi Kappa Phi has selected her for membership because of her dedication to education and higher learning.

A firm believer in professionalism, LilyB is one who truly lives her own philosophy - that to achieve, YA GOTTA BELIEVE!

## POSITIVE POWER PEOPLE
*The Enlightenment Amplifiers*

# YA GOTTA BELIEVE!

*By LilyB Moskal*

*"Do not follow where the path may lead.
Go, instead,
Where there is no path and leave a trail."
Anonymous*

SUCCESS IS NOT A DESTINATION BUT A CONTINUOUS JOURNEY SO....

...Come with me on a journey - a marvelous, exciting, adventurous journey to anywhere that is. Perhaps we will fly to the moon, or to the Milky Way or to the stars and planets beyond! We might plan to play a slow motion game of tennis or float weightless through time and space. It is possible, you know. Just about anything is possible today if you BELIEVE in it and are dedicated to it. For it has been said, "What the mind can conceive and believe, the mind can achieve."

It will be a glorious journey with new and exciting things happening to your life along the way. There will be, of course, detours along the way; stumbling blocks, rivers to cross, a mountain or two to climb for life's highway is constantly under construction. But no matter, for aren't the side trips of a journey sometimes surprisingly more interesting, more enjoyable than the journey itself? I have found it so.

Our journey will be an adventure in attitudes. An adventure that may be the turning point in your life. This very day you will, hopefully, decide to build a better you; to continue on this journey to a happier and more successful life.

*The Perfect Time*

But we must begin today - now - this very minute for today is that time when the future and the past meet. Do not look back - except to learn from past experiences - and do not spend needless time worrying about the past. Yesterday is a cancelled check, tomorrow a promissory note . . .only today is legal tender! Time is the only thing we each have equal amounts of, so use it wisely, productively, lovingly and guard it well for it is all we have.

So let's not waste any more precious time - let's get going on our journey into the future. The future being our lives. Are you ready? Good. Me too!

You may not realize it but you have already begun. Merely by picking up this book you have already taken the first step. For you are the people who can make things happen - for yourselves, your families, your businesses, your communities. YOU can mold this great world of ours. You and I have the opportunity, the responsibility, - yes, the POWER to make things happen. Things don't just happen. You have to MAKE them happen. Power people are merely those who are making positive things happen.

People, it is said, can be placed into three classes: the few who make things happen, the many who watch things happen and the overwhelming majority of those who don't even KNOW what's happening! In which class do you fit? In which class would you like to fit?

I feel certain we all wish to be successful, but what is success? Is there but one definition? I think not, for if each of us were asked, "What does success mean to you? What do you really want out of life?" I am sure we would all come up with different answers. We would probably hear words such as ACHIEVEMENT - ACCOMPLISH-MENT - FULFILLMENT - JOY - MONEY - LOVE. However, I believe that all of us wish to be happy. But happiness cannot be pursued like goals, for like a butterfly, it eludes you when you chase it, it will sometimes, when you least expect, come and light on your shoulder. Happiness comes with satisfaction - satisfaction with ourselves and with our work whatever it is. Of doing a job well; of doing and being the very best we can be.

*What Is Happiness?*

One of my favorite heroines said it this way. "Happiness cannot come from without. It must come from within. It is not what we see and touch or that which others do for us which makes us happy. It is that which we think and feel and do, first for the other fellow and then for ourselves." And who should know better than Helen Keller who lived all her life in a dark, sightless, soundless world. Yet she gave to mankind such riches, such inspiration, and values to live by. The story of her life and of her teacher, Ann Sullivan, who saw in Helen Keller the potential of greatness, is still an inspiration to me.

Yes, success means different things to different people. What motivates one may not motivate another but if Success and Happiness are achievable there is one word that describes a condition which will bring them about or keep us from having any of them, and that word is ATTITUDE!

Attitude can make the difference between success and failure, excellence and mediocrity, happiness and despair. It is profoundly significant that the only thing over which we have complete control is our own mental attitude. Our thinking apparatus belongs exclusively to us. No one can tell us what to think, but it is vitally important to our well being that we learn HOW to think! Albert Einstein said, "The reason so few people succeed is because men simply don't think." And I am sure he meant women as well!

*Where Action Begins*

Since all action begins with thought it is easily understood that everything that has ever happened in this world or will happen, began in one single brain cell in one human being. It is important that we understand and believe this and therefore know that we can change IF we want to, for success is no illusion. It is real and achievable and exists for everyone. Success, as well as happiness, can be yours if you BELIEVE that they can. We are better than we think we are, for we were born to choose, not to lose. I have the temerity to tell you that believing can lead to greater peace of mind and happiness as well as success in whatever field of endeavor you embark upon because it worked for me. It can work for you, but first - to borrow a phrase from that delightful character, Peter Pan - YA GOTTA BELIEVE!

What is it I am asking you to believe in? I am asking you to believe in yourself for we may succeed when others do not believe in us, but we can never be successful if we do not believe in ourselves. This is where our journey begins, and accomplishing it is the only way we can reach our destination - our goals.

All of us, unconsciously perhaps, want to feel good

about ourselves, but we do not always know quite how to go about it or where to start. Many do not know what to do about their situation. Tragically, unheeded by many, are such wise and timeless truths as said by Marcus Aurelius, "Very little is needed to make a happy life; it is all within yourself, in your way of thinking." Marcus, you were a wise man!

*Start With Love*

Eric Fromm and numerous other psychiatrists tell us that in order to like others we must first like ourselves. In fact, our ability to love - they say - stems from our ability to love ourselves. The Bible tells us: Love thy neighbor as thyself"... Not better than, nor less than, but AS thyself and the Bible's been around a long time!

How, though, do we learn to believe in ourselves, to feel good, to build an improved self image? In order to build good self esteem and thereby be the person we can be, acquiring the success we choose, we must have sufficient awareness to know what will make us feel good about ourselves, for herein lies the crucial need. We need a sense of self-worth, a sense of adequacy, and to obtain some degree of success. All our goals, our hopes and aspirations are based on this fundamental need.

We have compulsive needs - a desperate urge to love and be loved. To be accepted, approved, respected and looked up to, and if we examine the ultimate motivation back of such needs and urges we find it is our universal need to FEEL GOOD ABOUT OURSELVES!

*As You Think In Your Heart*

As a professional speaker traveling extensively and having the opportunity to meet and talk to many, many people in various walks of life, I am still, after years on the speaking circuit, amazed and somewhat dismayed at the poor attitudes and poor self images that prevail in the majority of people. Many still think of success as being lucky, having pull, knowing the right person, being born rich, or being crooked. It is not, nor has it ever been, any of these things. The formula for success is no secret but developing good, positive attitudes is the key!

Practically all man-made misery, emotional turmoil and suffering, is the product of limited and distorted awareness, of erroneous values, concepts and assumptions, and their ugly offspring, low-esteem. All lasting productive, constructive change in human systems starts with a changed image.

*Architects of Our Lives*

We are not the victims of circumstances - we are, rather, the architects of our lives. If we take complete and total responsibility for ourselves we can create the life that we really want. Nothing can keep you back if you mean to go forward!

A recent study by Stanford Research Institute concluded that 12% of our success depends on knowledge and 88% on the attitude and positive thinking of the individual. Ralph Waldo Emerson said, "We are what we think about all day long." He also said, "What lies behind us or what lies before us are tiny matters compared to what lies within us." And famed psychologist William James wrote: "The most amazing discovery of my generation is that people can alter their lives by merely altering their attitudes of mind."

My dear friend, Dr. Norman Vincent Peale, in his best seller: "The Power of Positive Thinking" writes:

*"Believe in yourself! Have faith in your abilities! Without a humble but reasonable confidence in your own powers you cannot be successful or happy. But with sound self-confidence you can succeed. A sense of inferiority and inadequacy interferes with the attain-*

*ment of your hopes, but self-confidence leads to self-realization and successful achievement...Mental attitude will help you believe in yourself and release your inner powers.* "

It is impossible to estimate the number of sales lost, businesses ruined, marriages failed, promotions missed by poor, negative attitudes. I am sure we all know of hundreds of jobs held but despised, marriages tolerated but unhappy, opportunities offered but not accepted, all because these people are waiting for others - the world - to change toward them instead of being big enough and wise enough to realize that we only get back what we are willing to put in. "As ye sow, so shall ye reap." Bitterness, anger, resentfulness can destroy those who harbor such negative feelings.

*Plant Good Crops*

With an improved self image comes self confidence, and self confidence is THE most valuable, most important asset a man or woman can possess. A self confident person is that person who knows and likes himself and therefore feels comfortable and at ease with others.

Don't you enjoy being around happy, optimistic, enthusiastic, positive people? Of course, we all do. You, too, can be that kind of person and when you are, others will want to be around you!

Think for a moment...picture in your mind someone whom you admire, whom you respect. The reason, I would venture to guess, is due to that person's good attitudes - first, about himself or herself and then about their world.

If you want to be great, be around great people. If you want to be successful, learn from successful people. Rub shoulders with them, ask them questions, find out what and how they think and to what they attribute their success.

Successful people realize their potential. They KNOW they have ability, and that they can succeed if they set reasonable, realistic, logical goals for themselves, have a continuing search for knowledge so that they learn more about their chosen profession every day, develop and improve skills and techniques. They are self motivated and are motivators of others. They radiate enthusiasm.

*Sunshine of Growth*

Enthusiasm is the greatest one word slogan for living ever devised. Enthusiasm glows...radiates...permeates and causes others to pay attention. Enthusiasm shines. It is that certain something that makes us great, that pulls us out of the mediocre and common place and builds into us power. Enthusiasm lights up our faces. It is the Keynote that makes us sing and makes others want to sing with us. It is the inspiration that makes us want to wake up and live. It puts spring in our step, joy in our hearts, a twinkle in our eyes and gives us confidence in ourselves and our fellow man. It changes a dead pan salesman into a producer, a pessimist into an optimist, a loafer to a go-getter. Enthusiasm is the producer of confidence that cries to the world, "I HAVE WHAT IT TAKES", without uttering a word to boast.

Remember that it is a person's ATTITUDE rather than his APTITUDE that determines his ALTITUDE! You may recall that wonderful song of the 40's that says it so well: YOU HAVE TO ACCENTUATE THE POSITIVE, ELIMINATE THE NEGATIVE, LATCH ON TO THE AFFIRMATIVE, AND DON'T MESS WITH MR. INBETWEEN!

*The Deep Waters*

Since the deepest urge of the human spirit is the desire

to be recognized, to be praised, to feel important, learn to compliment. "My, you look nice today." "That is a becoming color. You should wear it more often." "You did a fine job." Mark Twain said he could live for two months on one compliment. I can live for two years on one! A sincere, honest compliment will produce better results and is the best motivating factor of all. I know, for I learned this first hand a number of years ago, while trying to prepare breakfast for my four small children. The two boys, six and eight were eager to get off to school, my four year old daughter was crying because she couldn't go to school with her brothers and the baby was banging her cup on the highchair tray-table impatient for her breakfast, while I, in my old worn robe, stirred a big pot of grits. (We ate a lot of grits in those lean years, but still do because they are so GOOD!)

I was feeling very unappreciated, unloved, unhappy and sorry for myself as I served the grits onto the plates and splashed a big pat of butter in the middle of the creamy substance. I was feeling, as my mother would say, "lower than a snake's belly," when my little six year old looked up at me with big, brown velvet eyes 'and so innocently but sincerely said, "Momma, you sure are a good cooker!"

My - Oh, my! That old faded bathrobe became a red velvet mantle and I was, indeed, made queen for a day for I had been recognized, appreciated, praised. I now felt good - or at least better about myself all due to this little boy's sincere compliment over a mere plate of grits. I suddenly became a gourmet grits cooker! And it is still my claim to fame!

I hugged him and the others and was able to cope with the chores of the day more easily, for that compliment, given so sincerely, had helped make my day. You, too, can help make someone's day. If people do their job well, tell them so. Tell your children you are proud of them and they will try to live up to that expectation. Tell your spouse that you appreciate and love him-or her. They will find it easier to respond. The results can be excellent not only for the receiver but for the giver as well.

That same little boy became, at the age of 23, Louisiana's youngest State Representative. He is still helping people feel good about themselves, as are my other three children.

By making someone else feel good about themselves, you will also feel better about yourself...I guarantee - or as we say in my home state of Louisiana, I GAR RUN TEE! Ya Gotta Believe!

*The Harvest!*

All of us limit ourselves in some way or other and we reveal these limitations in the goals we set for ourselves and in the challenges we accept or reject.

You CAN be a winner; you were born to choose, not to lose. You can succeed if you first develop good, positive attitudes and set reasonable, reachable, realistic goals. You are YOUnique with different and various talents, abilities, and aptitudes.

It is never too late to remake your life on your own terms. Of course, there will be those stumbling blocks we mentioned earlier. Those rivers to cross and mountains to climb. But failure is only temporary - not permanent - unless we let it be. Failures are what build a person's character. It is not failure itself that causes us to fail, to give up, but our response to it, our reactions. No one drowns from falling into the water. He only drowns by staying there!

All of us, at one time or another, have failed, have been discouraged, disappointed, hurt, or depressed. No one ever promised us a rose garden without thorns! We do, however, have the power to think and the power of thought is becoming increasingly more noticed and respected, especially by the medical profession. Is it possible that love, hope, faith, laughter and the will to live a good life have therapeutic value? Do chemical changes occur only on the downside?

*Magic Healer*

Norman Cousins, editorial chairman of the Saturday Review and senior lecturer at the UCLA Medical School, asked these very questions laying in a hospital where doctors said he had one chance in 500 of recovering from ankylosing spondylitis. The connective tissue in his spine was gradually deteriorating. In a sense he was coming UNstuck. Cousins tells his remarkable yet believable story in his book ANATOMY OF AN ILLNESS AS PERCEIVED BY THE PATIENT. The first thing he did was move out of the hospital dropping much of his medication. Cousins figured laughter would contribute to positive attitudes so he got some films of Allen Funt's TV show, "Candid Camera" and some Charlie Chaplain and Marx Bros. movies and turned on the projector. It worked! He writes, "I made the joyous discovery that 10 minutes of genuine belly laughter had an anesthetic effect and would give me at least two hours of pain free sleep."

Over the months recovery came gradually but completely. On these spare details, it is a temptation to think you can cure whatever ails you with a few Marx Bros. movies and large doses of Vitamin C. There is naturally, more to it than that. Cousins, had, and has, an enormous will to live. He has one of the liveliest minds in American public life and his intellectual and moral power were turned loose against an invader in his body. It is what Dr. Albert Schweitzer called, the "inner doctor".

Remarkable? It happens every day. Humor - laughter - is good medicine, especially the ability to laugh at ourselves.

Yes, it happens every day to those who are determined

and who persevere, who refuse to lay back and die before they are dead, mentally as well as physically. Those who have the courage and the faith to believe - to believe in themselves and in their own power of positive thinking. We each have within us our own laser beam ...the light of life...a powerful force! Ya Gotta Believe!

*The New Season*

Growing and learning is a circular process: learning something new, making mistakes, failing, succeeding, gaining confidence, failing less of the time, succeeding, then off to new problems and adventures - new journeys. If the great inventors, scientists, leaders of our time did not dare to risk failure, to believe in themselves and their ability we would not live in the kind of world we so enjoy today.

No matter how meager your circumstances, how long a run of so-called bad luck you've experienced, how modestly nature has endowed you, you are YOUnique. You are the only one exactly like you. You can be proud about being yourself and humble about being only one among so many. So stretch - reach - grow!

Building self image and self confidence, like building an arch, takes some doing, but once you have it built, it is an architectural marvel and it can carry quite a load.

Taking responsibility for your life puts you in control. Events will no longer make you feel bad or good for it is how you decide to react to these events that will determine how you feel about them. You will look at your attitudes and beliefs in a more realistic light and change those that don't make any real sense. You will BELIEVE not only in yourself but in your ability to become successful.

## The Seeds of Life

Those of you who have read Richard Bach's beautiful book, Jonathan Livingston Seagull, will recall the point in the story where Jonathan, the gull, who dared to be different, who dared to want to fly higher and faster than any other, was ostracized from the flock. Thinking yourself in heaven he asked the great gull, Chiang, "Can you teach me to fly like that?" Jonathan Seagull trembled to conquer another unknown.

*"Of course, if you wish to learn."*
*"I wish. When can we start?"*
*"We could start now, if you'd like."*
*"I want to learn to fly like that," Jonathan said and a*
*strange light glowed in his eyes.*
*"Tell me what to do."*
Chiang spoke slowly and watched the younger gull ever so carefully.

*"To fly as fast as thought, to anywhere that is, you*
*must begin by BELIEVING that you have already*
*arrived..."*
I believe that a Jonathan Livingston Seagull lives in each of us ready to soar to unbelievable heights if we will just set him free...

*I have this feeling inside of me*
*To rise above the ordinary...*
*To be the person I'd like to be,*
*But, where do I start?*
*So much inside yearns to be heard,*
*Yearns to be free.*
*Yearns to share...to love...to be.*
*Where do I begin?*
*I suppose I begin with me.*

*YA GOTTA BELIEVE!*

*"When we say "I have lived" - every morning we arise we receive a bonus!"*
                    *Seneca*

"The Enlightenment Amplifiers"

**PEG BECKER**
Colonels Pride
Mt. Vernon, VA 22121
(703) 780-3595

## PEG BECKER

To "Keep History Alive" Peg Becker and her husband Dr. Arnold B. Becker donned costumes of George and Martha Washington, influenced by their dear friend Mrs. Bernice Carter Davis, author of "THROUGH THE WEST GATE OF MOUNT VERNON". Mrs. Davis had played the role of Martha many times but was aging and wished Peg to assume the character, then made Peg's first costume. Credit for much of this material is given to Mrs. Davis, learned through local folklore. Some stories came down through her family. Peg is the Great, Great Grandniece of Commodore "Saucy Jack Barry - First Admiral of our Navy".

The author has an impressive background in public health and Hospital Administration with Psychology and Speech at Harvard and Speech at Emerson College and Catholic University.

She is a member of the National Speakers Association and a Charter member of the National Capitol Speakers Association.

She was Mount Vernon - Lee Chamber of Commerce "Woman of the Year 1979" and has served on the Council of Little Theatre of Alexandria for twenty years.

The author says "Peg" stands for "People enjoy greatness" - the theme of many of her speeches.

**POSITIVE POWER PEOPLE**

# The Positive Power Of George Washington

*By Martha - As Portrayed by Peg Becker*

*"Behold his majestic fabric"* - Dryden

General George Washington was one of the greatest men who walked this earth - a man of positive power. He was a giant among men in stature (6 ft. 3 3/4 inches) and mind. The President of Harvard in that day considered him to be the best educated man in the world. It is said that he had such great martial dignity that it would set him apart from ten thousand men. Throughout Europe the rumor was spread that 'Not a king in Europe but would look like a Valet de Chambre by his side'. Mistress Abigail Adams on first meeting him rushed home to write to John who was at the Continental Congress in

Philadelphia 'Mind His Majestic Fabric' - a quote from the poet Dryden.

Ministers preached from the pulpit that his life had been spared at Fort Duquesne through Divine Providence for the service of his country.

Martha must have felt this as she stood resolutely and loyally by his side in eight long years of war and eight years of the Presidency.

It is my purpose to show that his positive power lay in his strong moral character and that he was programmed to greatness by his father.

Parents you will want to know this.

It is my fondest hope that all Americans will emulate his great example and from this will emerge great strong American leaders.

In 1982 we will be celebrating the 250th Anniversary of his birth on February 22, 1732.

We must express and dramatize the events of his life as a new nation emerges so the young people and parents of today will understand the making of his great positive power.

We need a nation of honest, strong Americans.

We must clothe the Father of our Country in flesh and blood. George Washington was abundantly human.

*Go - Washington - Go!*

Will you tell the youth of our Country of the positive power of a fifteen year old teenager named George Washington who signed his name "Go. Washington!" This could have been his positive power motivator - a positive affirmation dropped into his subconscious every time he signed his name. We wonder if he said to himself Go Washington, Go!

At fifteen he assisted John West to survey and lay out the city lots, roads and market place of Alexandria, Va., auctioning off lots at six pistoles ($30.00). Through

George Washington's hard work this herculean task was completed in four months. The original grid has the lot owner's names in George Washington's handwriting. He had learned geometry, trigonometry and surveying from his father and inherited his instruments. This was the first hard cash George Washington received. The only people of that day who received hard cash were surveyors. Hard money was positive power when there was little of it. He was ambitious and worked long hours. It is said he ran with his lines. Within two years he was considered one of the most honest and accurate of surveyors. He wrote the deeds and recorded them. Most of the conflicts between colonists came from inaccurate surveys.

At the age of seventeen he presented himself at Culpepper Court House to apply for the position of Chief Surveyor for the County. He asked for what he wanted. Go, Washington, Go! Royal Governor Dinwiddie of Virginia appointed him to the post. This put him in a positive power position. His fortunes improved. The next day he earned thirty-seven dollars net after he and his assistants surveyed a four hundred acre tract. This was a hundred times the pay of a farm worker. Within that year he bought 1500 acres of prime land in the Shenandoah Valley. Go, Washington, Go!

That year his brother Lawrence died leaving him Mount Vernon. He was now a landowner of importance and a person of substance in his community. (Go, Washington, Go!)

He set a goal (one of his positive powers) to continue surveying for the next three years and triple his land holdings. (Go, Washington, Go!) He also had a goal to serve his country so he applied for his brother's Commission as Major and Adjutant of the Colonial Militia. He received it. Later he served as an Aide to General Braddock. His positive power was to be ready for his opportunity when it came. He had made rounds with his brother who spent time schooling him in martial arts.

He had been taught to fence, drill and take command, as well as military science.

Will you tell of his deeds of valor in the Campaign's of the French and Indian Wars?

How at Fort Duquesne two horses were shot from under him. There were four bullet holes in his coat and his hat was shot off. All the other officers were picked off including General Braddock who died. George took command, rallied the troops and led them to safety. During the battle he had ridden between two firing columns striking up the guns with his sword, with no thought of his personal safety. He seemed invulnerable to bullets. He wondered about this and wrote in his diary "The Miraculous Care of Providence...protected me beyond all human expectation'.

*He Became a National Hero*

He was promoted to Commander-in-Chief of the Frontier Forces of Virginia at twenty-two. (Go, Washington, Go!)

After receiving a vote of thanks from the Virginia Assembly for his heroism at Fort Duquesne, he rose as if to respond and didn't say a word. The Speaker of the House is quoted as saying, "Mr. Washington, your valor only exceeds your modesty and that surpasses any power of any language I possess". One of General George Washington's greatest positive powers was knowing when not to speak.

> James 3:2 "If anyone can control his tongue, it proves that he has perfect control over himself in every other way".

Will you tell about the Country Squire who turned his father's eight room house on the Potomac into a twenty-two room mansion with a piazza? It took him twenty years to realize this goal. Tenacity of purpose was another of his positive powers.

The Father of Your Country rose at four doing hours of office work and writing in his diary before breakfast.

At twenty-six he led a peaceful life of great domestic felicity with Martha his good and understanding wife. This was to have been his ultimate goal - but fate decided otherwise.

Can you tell of a country gentlemen whose hospitality was unsurpassed, whose friends were a positive power to him? His mansion was filled with house guests. His board groaned with roast wild turkey, Sally Lunn, rich thick peanut soup and Martha's famous cakes. Great bowls of mint julep graced his buffet. He lived the life for which he had always yearned. He was living a life of self-fulfillment. This charming host always gave thanks to the source of his power and would make his earnest toast to the ladies and gentlemen.

> *"To - Our Land Free.*
> *To - Our men Honest.*
> *To - Our women Fruitful."*

Shortly after Patrick Henry had proclaimed "Give me Liberty or Give me Death" tempers were running high. Many of George Washington's Tory neighbors who sympathized with the Crown considered him to be the firebrand of the beginning Revolution. He was chasing a fox through one such Tory's land - this gentleman appeared with a shot gun aimed at George. George tossed his gun to his negro riding behind him and shouted "If he kills me - you kill him" and rode away after the fox. He led a charmed life.

It is my earnest hope that savory bits of history of his great positive powers will be on the lips of all during the 250th Anniversary and that we will all learn to use the great power the Father of our Country possessed.

*Boyhood Influences*

The story of the cherry tree was true. George admitted

to the deed and Parson Weems embroidered the tale with literary license. However, many an American child has been motivated to be courageously truthful by "I can not tell a lie".

George Washington was the first son of August (Augustine) Washington's second marriage. He was the apple of his father's eye and resembled him in stature and calmness of disposition. August wanted to keep George by his side and tutor him and teach him the ways of the world rather than have him exposed to outside influences. They lived in rural isolation with no schools, no nearby children or older members of the family who might exert a bad influence. August had been a sheriff and now was a judge who had been given the title of Captain for his many years of honest and incorruptible service. He was a man of honor and integrity in his community.

Contrary to what we believe, the Washingtons were not rich nor did they lead the social life of the wealthy planters of that day. They owned twenty slaves. Ten were able-bodied and five were totally incapacitated. They had warm clothes and enough to eat but lived a spartan existence with few of the amenities of life. George and his father worked in the fields with "their people" as they called the negroes. His mother had five children in quick succession. Although she was a hard worker she was overburdened.

It was most important to August to buy more land so as to give each of his sons an inheritance. He bought the Ferry Farm in Fredericksburg in addition to Mount Vernon and the Pope's Creek Farm where George was born. He was an ambitious man - ambitious for his sons in whom he had great hope. It was important to him to keep his two older sons, Lawrence and Austin (Augustine, Jr.) by his first marriage, in Appleby School - one of the finest in England. August had attended this school and knew the headmaster. When George was five his father spent a year at Appleby School in England learning to tutor

George for whom he had the highest hopes and expectations. Lawrence and Austin (Augustine, Jr.) had been attending this school for some time. He had not seen them for years and was delighted with their progress. They were two manly young men with great poise. They were of honest, forthright moral character with keen progressive minds. Later they were to tutor George when his father died. Royalty attended this school. The great Samuel Johnson had aspired to be headmaster here but was not accepted, so high were the standards. The professors were Greek and Latin scholars who inspired the boys in all the noble qualities of sterling character and leadership of the ancient Greeks and Romans before the corrupt age of the Caesars. They were schooled in the great military campaigns, the science of government and dedication to the service of one's Country. Noble leaders gave their services to the State without remuneration, (General and President Washington later did this). All this was brought home to George. The accent was on the individual's nobility of character in leadership, later his great positive power. Years later General Washington exhorted his fellow citizens to develop these qualities and signed it Go, Washington.

## "WASHINGTON'S LEGACY"

*"I now make it my earnest prayer, that God would have you, and the State over which you preside, in his holy protection, that he would incline the hearts of the Citizens to cultivate a spirit of subordination and obedience to Government, to entertain a brotherly affection and love for one another, for their fellow Citizens of the United States at large, and particularly for their brethren who have served in the Field, and finally, that he would most graciously be pleased to dispose us all, to do justice, to love mercy, and to demean ourselves with that Charity, humility and pacific temper of mind, which were the*

*Characteristics of the Divine Author of our blessed Religion, and without an humble imitation of whose example in these things, we can never hope to be a happy Nation.* "

*Go, Washington*

## RULES WHICH CONCERN CONDUCT

Do not laugh too loud or too much in company.

Let your discourse with men of business be short and comprehensive.

Do not laugh at your own witticisms.

Show good example. Particularly before the less experienced.

Do not give advice unless you are asked.

Be not curious to know the affairs of others.

Do not contradict at every turn the statements others make.

Point not with thy finger.

Good humor makes one dish of meat a feast.

August Washington sought only that the right thoughts were put into George's mind. Positive Power Affirmations and good examples of his father were the source of his strong moral character. August programmed him to greatness.

The subconscious mind is a source of positive power. It can be likened to a computer - what is fed in-comes out. The subconscious mind is capable of doing more. It is related to the spirit - the soul. It is the core of positive power that can make you be what you should be, act as you want to act and accomplish what you want to accomplish from life-if you keep free of negative thoughts and actions and have complete conscious control of it. George Washington governed his own life and further spiritualized it.

Many times he copied and memorized this excerpt from the Reverend Thomas Comber's Discourses.

"Prayer is the lifting up of the soul to converse with God, and a means to obtain all his blessings."

We see General George Washington on his knees at Valley Forge beseeching the Almighty.

Douglas Southall Freeman, the great historian of Washington stated:

"His continuing commission, never outdated, was that of self command."

Captain Washington was his son's principal tutor in his early years. George Washington's copy books are in the Library of Congress. His exercises in penmanship were copying The Code of Conduct From Appleby (also called The Code of Civility and Hawkin's Rules). George called it "The Rules of Civility and Decent Behavior in Company and Conversation". Copies of Hawkins Rules may be found in The British Museum in London. They were said to be a bridge between the Ten Commandments and the Bible. The rules were copies over and over - all 119 of them, and memorized. With the Ten Commandments and the Bible they sank deep into George's life and became his guiding light - one of the sources of his positive power.

His mother was quick with the switch and saw to it he rigidly adhered to the Rules. No negative back talk was allowed to come to rest in his mind. Obedience without question and trust in his Father and complete honesty were the law of the household. There were no negative forces here. The household worked for one common goal, to get ahead in life.

All of the great men of Europe were educated by these precepts. William Pitt who became Prime Minister of England at twenty-four was educated in this manner.

Even the little Mozart who wrote his first Sonata at eight years was heard to murmur "After God, Papa". George Washington was mature and wise beyond his years. These Rules, all Positive Power Affirmations were dropped into his subconscious mind for ready recall when the occasion demanded.

His conscious mind was in complete control of his subconscious mind. No temptations or negative thoughts were allowed to enter. George was positively self influenced.

## RULES WHICH TAUGHT CHARACTER

Associate yourself with persons of good character.
It is better to be alone than in bad company.
Think before you speak.
Accept corrections thankfully.
Be not obstinate in supporting your own opinions.
Treat sublime matters seriously.
Do not repeat news if you do not know the truth there-of.
Speak no evil of the absent.
When you speak of God and his attributes, let it be seriously and with reverence.
Honor and obey your natural parents even though they be poor.
Let your recreations be manly not sinful.
Labor to keep alive in your breast that little spark of celestial fire called conscience.

## RULES FOR CONSIDERATION OF OTHERS

Do not hum or drum with your hands or feet when in company.
Do not reprove or correct another in anger.
Do not curse or revile anyone.
Let your conversation be without malice or envy.
Yield the place in front of the fire to the latest comer.
Jog not the desk at which another reads or writes.
Do not read the writing or books of another unless asked to do so.

Speak not injurious words in jest or in earnest.
In disputes give liberty to each to resent his opinion.
Be attentive when others speak.
If you cough, sneeze, sigh or yawn do it privately.

## RULES THAT URGE MODESTY

Always submit your judgements to others with modesty.
Do not undertake to teach your equal in an act in which he is qualified.
Be modest in your apparel! Do not play the peacock.
Do not fuss with your clothing in public or constantly check your shoes, your stockings, etc.
A man should not preen himself about his achievements, his wit, his virtue and much less his wealth.
Laugh not loudly or at all without occasion.

## RULES THAT ADVISED COMPASSION

When a man does the best he can, yet succeeds not, do not blame him.
Do not express joy before one who is sick or in pain.
Show not yourself glad at another's misfortune.
Reproach none for the infirmities of nature.

## RULES THAT ENFORCE RESPECT FOR ELDERS AND PERSONS IN POSITIONS OF AUTHORITY AND RESPONSIBILITY

Show respect to people of distinction, to judges and ministers. If anyone comes to speak to you while you are sitting, stand up even though you consider him to be your inferior.
If you meet a person who is your elder, yield to him the path or right of way.

In speaking give everyone his due title.

When your superiors are talking - do not speak or laugh.

When your elders are talking speak not until you are asked a question. Then stand up and answer in a few words.

*"Let us see to it that our lives, like jewels of great price, be noteworthy not because of their width, but because of their weight."*

   *Seneca*

**LARRY WESTERMAN**
4062 Caminito Dehesa
San Diego, CA 92107
(714) 226-0053

## LARRY WESTERMAN

Larry Westerman, author of "The Power is Within," was once described by a friend as the man who had taken the most self-improvement classes in San Diego.

For the past five years, he has turned this experience around to become one of the city's most in-demand speakers and motivators. Larry is co-founder of the Professional Speakers Association of San Diego and a member of the National Speakers Association. He began teaching sales techniques and motivation to his co-workers at Realty World and then, in 1978, went on to form his own company, AIM YOUR POTENTIAL. From this base, Larry and his staff have spoken to hundreds of civic, social and business organizations on topics of non-verbal communication, stress release, motivation, behavior modification and self-hypnosis.

Westerman has a B.A. degree from San Diego State University and is currently a doctoral candidate in psychology. He served as President of the Academic Resource Center for five years and four years headed the National Programmed Learning Institute.

In 1979, the author was selected by the Sales and Marketing Executive Club of San Diego for their 1978 Distinguished Salesman Award, in recognition of his work in hypnosis and his ability to teach others sales psychology.

4

POSITIVE
POWER
PEOPLE
*The Enlightenment Amplifiers*

# THE POWER IS WITHIN

*By Larry Westerman*

*"There is no such thing as a problem without a gift for you in its hands......"*
*Richard Bach - Illusions*

Most adolescents manage to go through a terrible identity crisis from which they emerge knowing who they are and where they are going. Somehow I missed this natural maturational process in my teens and arrived at the age of 38 before plunging headlong into an identity crisis which lasted fifteen months. While those were the darkest months in my life, I wouldn't have traded them for anything, because I emerged from that dark night of the soul into a light that puts everything I encounter into a bright perspective.

## My Personal Pearl Harbor

On December 7th - more than a quarter century after the bombing of Pearl Harbor - my companion of two years dropped a huge, lethal bombshell on our relationship. I was devastated. I sank into a dark despair that seemed just as permanent as the mud at the bottom of Pearl Harbor.

Now, to the casual observer who imagined he knew me, I did not seem particularly "devastatable." I appeared to be a success and to "have my act together." As a student, I was always in the top third of my class; in the Navy, I was an officer and pilot. As a businessman I had also proved successful, first as head of a private adult school, and then in real estate sales and management. I dressed well and radiated assurance; my outward appearance mirrored my material prosperity. Underneath this facade, however, was an emotional adolescent, striking out in pain and anger against this terrible, unlooked-for rejection.

## Look Within

There was one thing I had going for me though that the average adolescent - or even the average adult - did not: I had learned to look for the answer within. One day, about thirteen years before this trauma, I was riding my bike. It was trash day. As I rode by a very full trash can perched precariously on the curb, I saw a couple of record albums on the top of the heap. I stopped and went back to investigate. The covers featured the names of no recording artists of whom I had ever heard. The records, by Douglas Edwards and Cavett Robert were on sales motivation and techniques. Here I was in sales at the time and I didn't even know such aids existed!

I rescued the records from certain burial and knocked

on the door of the nearest house. Yes, it was the trash can owner. No, she didn't mind if I took the records. They had belonged to her recently-deceased sister who had sold real estate. There had been more records like these but she had donated them to a thrift store. She couldn't remember which one. I spent several hours combing through the records of every thrift store in San Diego without discovering the rest of the late real estate woman's collection. However, the two treasures that I had found opened doors into my mind that I never knew existed and started me on an inward search that has continued ever since.

*Learn - Learn - Learn*

For the next thirteen years I took every class I could find in self-improvement, motivation and hypnosis. Friends would introduce me as the man who had taken the most self-improvement classes in San Diego - and they were probably correct. Everything I learned was useful to me, but somehow it never all came together. Door after door was opening, but down at the bottom of the stairs of my mind was one solid oak door that was still locked. I knew I was moving; I just didn't know where. It took this traumatic undoing of a relationship to force me to start looking for my own answer, my own way, my own special key.

Despite the apparent smoothness of my life, I always had felt a continual nagging of self doubt. I felt somehow younger than my associates - four years younger to be exact. "If only I was four years older I could fly better," I would say to myself. In a similar vein, if someone complimented me, I didn't believe it was sincere and couldn't accept a compliment graciously. There would be this nagging thought: "Why did they say that? What do they want from me?" Frequently I was praised for my potential. To me that was like giving a medal to a high diver who was still standing on the diving board, looking down at the water. And there was another area of my life which reflected my uncertainty about what the world would hold for me. No matter how much I earned, I was always chasing my checkbook, never sure whether I would make it or not.

*Look For The Gift*

I knew that Clement Stone had said, "In every adversity there is a seed of good." That's what I always pictured - a seed. Not a seed sprouting and giving birth to a lush, green plant, but just a seed, sitting there and being a seed. It wasn't until I read Bach's ILLUSIONS and could substitute the image of a gift within a problem rather than a seed that I was able to probe adversity looking for good.

So there I was, 38 years old, dumped and miserable, yet with thirteen years of resource material stored within me. Finally I was forced to come to terms with unhappy feelings that had plagued me all my life but until that point had been able to suppress. There was no way I could do that any longer. I had to probe the pain and seek the gift.

*The Chrome Ring in My Mind*

For three months I ached, thought and sought. I meditated by the swimming pool and each night walked from 11 p.m. to 1 a.m. so that I would be tired enough to sleep. One evening, on one of these long walks, my mind presented me with a symbol which was to show me the answer to my problems. In my hypnosis classes I had learned that the brain is composed of two hemispheres. One of these, the dominant hemisphere, controls our practical and logical thinking. The other, the non-dominant, controls our creative side and our dreams. It was this, non-dominant, part of my mind which presented me with a clear image.

Suddenly, in my mind, I saw an unusual, beautiful chrome ring. The word "me" was in the center and there were four breaks in it. If the ring were the face of a clock, the breaks appeared at three, six, nine and twelve. At each break there was a significant name: my father's name was at noon, the high point; my sister's at three o'clock; the girlfriend whose recent rejection had thrown me into despair, at six; and my ex-wife's at nine.

I immediately understood the message of this symbol my mind had presented to me. Even though my most recent break was with my girlfriend, I had to make things right with my father, sister and former wife as well. Only when I had repaired all four breaks in this ring could I become the whole person I knew I was intended to be. The gaps in these relationships were inside me and the potential for healing them was inside me as well. When the ring was made whole, I would find the maturity and feeling of well being I had always longed for.

## My Sister

I decided that I would begin to mend the chrome ring by reaching an accord with my sister. Right or wrong, I had grown up with a tremendous feeling of resentment against my younger sibling. I perceived her as being smarter than I and Father's favorite. I had felt overshadowed by her throughout my childhood and had never really gotten over this feeling as an adult.

My sister and her husband were taken by surprise when I called them in Los Angeles and announced I wanted to take Melna out to dinner. Knowing my mental state at the time, she had a certain amount of reservation about spending time alone with me, especially in view of our relationship over the years. I reassured her by telling her she could pick out the restaurant where we would go. In Los Angeles there are probably about 1000 good restaurants to choose from so I was really amazed when she selected one, forty-five minutes drive from her home, that I had previously picked out as the restaurant to which I wanted to take her. Also, this was a place where we had never been together. I looked at her choice as an auspicious beginning.

That evening was incredible. We sat, ate and talked for four hours. I admitted to her all the thoughts and feelings I had harbored against her since childhood. I had never opened up to her like this before. She said very little in response, however, and on the flight back to San Diego I began to worry that maybe I had done the wrong thing. Then, a couple of days later, a beautiful letter from Melna arrived. In it she told me that it was easier for her to express herself in writing. She let me know that she valued greatly my honesty that evening and, as I read her letter, the old remaining shreds of my negative feelings toward her magically dissolved. I remember that she wrote, "Now I can see why people say you're so warm." Until that evening, I hadn't showed the warmth to my sister that it was easy to lavish on mere acquaintances.

Today, my sister and I have an extremely satisfactory relationship. This doesn't mean that we think and act alike. We are two very different people. But the evening I took the risk of opening myself up to her taught me that I was O.K., just as she was O.K. I accept her for the unique person she is and find I can value my own uniqueness as well.

## My Father

Ever since I can remember there has been a strained coolness in my relationship with my father. I knew it originated with me and in no way reflected on the unconditional love and kindness he had always showered on me. If anything, his care for me bordered on being embarrassing, such as the time when he asked my superior officer to take good care of me before my squadron was shipped overseas. I knew that my father loved me and that there was nothing he wouldn't give me or do for me. That's why I felt particularly guilty about my aloofness toward him.

Now that I had the ring to guide me, bridging the gap would be easy. After all, it should have been harder to approach my sister, toward whom I had always felt such jealousy, than my always loving and giving father. But the harder I tried to express loving feelings to him, the worse I felt. There was a core of rejection of him inside me that made me feel like a terrible son. I discovered this wasn't the sort of problem that could be talked out in one four-hour dinner at a nice restaurant. In all honesty, I didn't even know what the problem was. All I knew was that there was a feeling of reserve deep down within me and whenever I tried to communicate with my father, the coldness was there.

One evening, I was enjoying a walk along Mission Bay with my good friend, Paula Sullivan. Paula is a wise, wonderful woman, a few years older than I, who has seen me through some of the rough times in my life. It was a beautiful moon-lit evening and we were thoroughly enjoying our stroll and conversation. I was telling her about my two children, Tom and Anne, who were then twelve and six. There were no two people on earth I loved more deeply than my children. They had just spent a wonderful weekend with me and had returned a couple of hours earlier to their mother's home.

### Enlightenment

It was then that Paula casually asked an innocent question that illuminated the dark recesses of my childhood memories. The darkness around me literally lit up as though with a blaze of the noonday sun. All of a sudden I knew the reason for my coolness toward my father and why it was unfounded. Taken out of context, Paula's question may seem a bit strange, but it followed quite naturally in the discussion about my children's visit. "Where do your children sleep when they come to visit you?" Paula asked.

Since the divorce, the children had always taken turns sleeping with me when we were together. We all appreciated this special opportunity to cuddle together and share our warmth and love. Sharing closeness seemed a very natural thing and warm physical contact was something I had grown to believe all parents should have with their children.

As I started to reply to Paula's question, the light dawned. Suddenly, I was reminded of a shocking and unpleasant experience that I had as a boy of nine. My parents ran a summer resort and one of the guests had forced me into a homosexual activity. I was mortified and could not tell my father what had happened. Fortunately, the man also made amorous advances toward some of the women guests and my father swiftly sent him packing. I was greatly relieved that he was gone but could never bring myself to tell anyone what had happened. My deeply buried feelings of shame and rage, however, translated into unconscious anger toward older men - including my father.

A few years later, a death in my Father's family caused us all to travel to the East Coast. On the trip back to California, my father and I shared a motel room and a bed. My father cuddled me before he fell asleep, in the same way I now cuddle with my own children, but because of my experience with the molester, I misunderstood his caresses. Each night after he fell asleep, I lay awake in the bed, confused, angry and terribly afraid.

Now, finally, I understood that my father had loved

and cuddled me in the same pure, fatherly fashion I loved and cuddled my children. I could now look on that negative experience as a nine year old from the perspective of a mature adult. I had been confusing a traumatic sexual experience with a stranger with loving, physical contact with my father.

Once I had literally seen the light, it was easy to approach my father with a new appreciation. I followed the advice I had heard Cavett Robert give at a sales rally. I went to my father and said, "Dad, you know we are both getting on in years now and there is no saying how much time we'll have together - so let's talk and get to know each other better."

The gap at the high noon point on the ring was completely mended. Since my father died of cancer only two years later, I was particularly grateful for the insight I needed to make things right between us. Thank you, Mind!

## *My Girlfriend*

This relationship was to take a different kind of healing. I was totally infatuated with her and she would have nothing to do with me. I would actually spend hours during my floortime in the real estate office simply staring out the door, hoping she would drive by. She had no cause to be in that neighborhood and never, in all my hours of staring, did I catch a glimpse of her. My letters to her were returned unopened and her new phone number unlisted.

I finally came to realize that the gap in the ring representing our relationship was one that needed only my healing. After all, she was apparently not going around feeling miserable. She wasn't lingering, hoping to catch a sight of me in my car. Her life had not come to an abrupt end when we split up, as had mine.

It took fifteen months for me to realize that the relationship itself would not mend, that I could heal the gap in the ring only by letting go. In the process, I learned that I was a complete person in and of myself and didn't require another person's love to function in the world. The gift I found in this problem was a new self-respect, independence and the knowledge that I, and no one else, was my responsibility.

I worked on myself, using the self-hypnosis and visualization techniques that I was teaching to others. One day I took a peek at the imaginary ring my mind had given me and the gap at six o'clock was smoothly mended.

## My Ex-Wife

My relationship with my ex-wife has been the most difficult to heal. There was no longer love between us, as there had been with my sister and father, yet she was a continuing presence in my life because of the children we both loved and shared. Even as I write this, the section of the ring symbolizing our relationship appears to have an awkward soldering job, as opposed to the completely smooth continuity of the chrome at the other points, and will probably remain rough until our children are grown.

To acquire even the soldering effect, I have had to accept that although I no longer love - or even like - her, she is due my respect as the mother of my children and as a unique person in her own right. In honestly accepting my feelings about her, I no longer need be bothered by old scripts, guilts and anger that could have a negative effect on our children.

## The Ring Made Whole

It has been three years since my mind showed me the

chrome ring and how to heal it. Part of that process was a searching personal inventory, more intensive than I had ever attempted before. I set goals for myself in seven important areas of living: spiritual, family, financial, social, physical, mental and education. It has been wonderful to see how these areas work together and support each other when all are fostered.

Since that time, I left real estate sales and formed my own company, "AIM YOUR POTENTIAL", a successful business which has helped many people become more motivated and effective.

As a result of many public appearances, I became known as an expert on body language and non-verbal communication and this is what brought Diana into my life. She came into my office one day to ask me to speak before a group, the Women's Council of Realtors. We had a three hour lunch and soon were seeing each other regularly. Diana shared her spiritual beliefs with me and I went with her to the La Jolla Church of Religious Science to hear a dynamic minister, Rev. Terry Cole-Whitaker. The spiritual side of my life, hitherto undernourished, began to bloom as I learned about the universal laws of metaphysics.

Most important, with Diana, I discovered a capacity within myself to love and care with an intensity I never knew before. Through the gift of the ring, I had learned to solve the problems in prior relationships and I had a whole self to bring to this new one.

The end of the quotation from ILLUSIONS which preceeds this little story is:

*"You seek problems because you need their gifts."*

There are no coincidences. The thirteen years I had spent in preparation enabled me to look within for the gift from my personal Pearl Harbor. I knew the power was within and was given the opportunity to use it. That same power is within the mind of each and every one of us, waiting to give us the unimaginable gift of ourselves.

*"As long as you live, keep learning how to live."*
*Seneca*

The Enlightenment Amplifiers

JUNE FULCHER
2111 Business Center Dr.
Suite 240
Irvine, California 92715
(714) 955-1491

## JUNE FULCHER

June Fulcher is the president of the successful nation-wide Venus de Milo chain. Married to husband Jack, they have two grown children and their first grandchild, Grant.

At age 30 June made Jesus Christ Lord and Master of her life. Since then He has taken her and her family from nothing to ownership of a multi-million dollar corporation in 10 years.

On faith she, her husband, and sister Sussie, opened the first Venus de Milo Salon in Yuma, Arizona. There are now over 180 salons nation-wide and opening 6 to 7 new ones every month.

June is an energetic, petite, business woman who loves what she is doing and loves people. However, at one time she too had a weight problem. Her "before" statistics are: height 5' 2 3/4" weight 139. She is now: height 5' 2 3/4" and weighs 110 lbs.

After living in California for several years, she now lives in Texas where she was born and raised, ...travels around the country for Venus, and when in Irvine, California, puts regular hours in at corporate offices located there.

"Following God's Word daily, prayer, hard work and total commitment is my answer. God, and total submission to Him, is my secret weapon," stated June.

A dynamic, outgoing lady, June is a welcome addition to any speaker's platform or talk show.

**5**

POSITIVE
POWER
PEOPLE

*The Enlightenment Amplifiers*

# THE POWER OF INNER BEAUTY

*By June Fulcher*

*Psalm 111:10: "The fear of the Lord is the beginning of wisdom; a good understanding have all they that do His commandments; His praise endureth forever."*

Sussie and I stood inside our very first Venus de Milo Salon. Standing on faith, on a dream and just a little scared. My sister Sussie, husband Jack, kids, dogs and cats had left security, a job, sold everything and moved to Yuma, Arizona based on a late night dream.

### The Dream

I saw myself standing on a lovely street corner. The sidewalk was so hot that I felt the heat burning all the way to my knees. In looking around, instead of street signs I saw a map and I knew I was standing in the corner of three states; Arizona, New Mexico and California. Sussie and Jack were there, yet I knew the dream was mine. I tried to question God's message to me. The next morning I felt a glow of peace, excitement and anticipation and I couldn't wait to share with Jack and Sussie. They were so open and receptive that I knew it was from God; the answer to a prayer. We got a map of the western United States and we all felt God was showing us Yuma, Arizona. We prayed together and in total faith Jack quit his Civil Service job; we had a total of $8,000. We packed our belongings in a rental trailer and, with our kids, moved to Yuma, Arizona. When we arrived we drove to the center of town. I saw my street corner and in the middle of July when I stepped out of the car onto the sidewalk, the heat burned all the way to my knees! Now, just 3 months later, Sussie and I waited for our first customer. Jack was taking care of our children and our books, and we were completely broke.

Our door began to open, a very large woman and her daughter started to walk in, they looked around and then began to back out again. I ran after them, touched the woman on the arm, saying "Don't be afraid. I've been fat, too, I know how to help you. Just let me show you how our system works." They came back in and we signed our first two clients for $68.00 in October of 1969. We took the money and bought groceries and were reminded of Philippians 4:19, "And my God shall supply all your needs according to His riches in glory in Christ Jesus." (New American Standard)

Now, I'm not a lucky person, an unusually smart person or an especially hard worker. I am a very blessed person. I know that I am where I am because God gave it all to me. How else would a housewife from Texas become the founder of a multi-million dollar, nationwide corporation?

I've heard many people who have achieved success of one kind or another say they didn't know how or why it happened to them. For me, it was the day I totally submitted my life to God, gave up my right to choose. Oh, I had gone to a church as a child, in fact, in our small town church was the entertainment, music, socials and dinners out. I had an acquaintance with Jesus Christ, but He was not Lord of my life until age 30. My husband Jack accepted Christ just two weeks later. Now, I grew up believing Christians were supposed to be ugly, poor and sour pusses, and I didn't want that, so I began demanding of God. "Father, I want this and I want that and don't give me any of those!"

I had two small children and I became one of the first 10 sales girls for Mary Kay Cosmetics. Out of a small town of 4,000 I then became one of her top 10 sales ladies and when I had gone as far as I could, I wanted more. I told God I wanted out, I wanted money and He had better do something NOW!

## Turning Point

As I prayed that morning, I began to really listen to myself, how I was talking to God, my Father in heaven. Then I knelt before my Lord seeking forgiveness and that day in my bedroom I asked God to be Master of my life, submitting myself, my marriage, my children and home to Him. From the depths of my heart I prayed that whatever and wherever He wanted me, I would do and be. If He wanted me to stay at home - live and die in this little house - then I would and I would make it the best home possible to honor Him. I just wanted His perfect will in my life.

## The Beginning

Within a month our house sold and we relocated because of my husband's job. In 1967 I became the manager of a health club. I went in looking for just a job and was given the position of manager. My husband had been teaching me about exercise since I was 20 years old. Because I had a very real weight problem (5'2 and 3/4 inches and 139 pounds), I had learned a great deal about diet by just trial and error. After being at the health club for only a short time, I went from 139 pounds to 110 pounds; a loss of 29 pounds and 22 inches. As I look back now I know God was preparing me for Venus de Milo. The owner of the health club wanted me to be in charge of the six outlets he owned, but I turned him down. We wanted to move and I knew God had something else for me.

Sussie, my beloved sister, and her children came to live with us and all of us prayed about what God wanted for our families. Sussie's marriage had just failed and she was sure she, too, was a failure. She had never worked, had no experience of any kind and children to raise. They came to live with us since she and I had always been close. Sussie had always had an easier relationship with the Lord, a more accepting nature, but this was a hard time and she couldn't find work. Finally, Sussie got a job with a dry cleaner with no breaks of any kind. So I took lunch to her every day until she was able to come to work with me at the health club. She sold $4,000 in cosmetics each month that first year and we all saved money, knowing there was something more for all of us.

Then came my dream and our plans fell into place. with faith and a positive step forward, we committed to God and put our trust into action.

### About Venus

Venus de Milo is a figure control and reducing salon uniquely tailored to meet the needs of every female figure of any age. Venus specializes in individual attention to each of the ladies. Sooner or later, every woman needs the Venus de Milo Way in her life. As one client said, "I feel so special and wanted here. It is my own 'little fuzzy' to carry all day long."

Included in the program is non-passive exercise equipment and a doctor approved diet. From the very first, we got weight off and kept it off, so the word spread.

We do not have long term memberships or contracts. There are no hidden costs and all our salons are owned and managed by "ex-fatties". Therefore, they thoroughly understand how ugly fat is and can genuinely sympathize with client friends who are struggling to lose weight.

Our program is designed to reduce weight and inches, increase lung supply and strengthen the heart. All this without starving your pocketbook. Our ladies not only look better, but feel better too, and our program is for ladies of all ages.

And that first day in Yuma is repeated over and over again. A lady will start to come in, see our skinny owners, and a look of terror will come into her eyes as she starts to back out the door. This happens because quite often with over-weight there is a lack of self-esteem; a fear that you are really not feminine or desirable. And so, you feel a need to hide inside yourself.

*God Doesn't Make Junk*

We want our ladies to feel good about themselves, to see themselves as they can be. So we make sure that the ladies know we understand. Over and over we'll say, "I know, I used to be overweight myself and I know I can help you. Here, let me show you my 'before' and'after' pictures." Then we just talk over a cup of coffee or tea about feelings; how it feels to be overweight and that helps open the door to hope.

Because we know by experience that the system works, we do offer hope. Because we all really care about our clients, we offer genuine interest, encouragement and lots of TLC - Tender Loving Care.

An 83 year old lady comes in every day and insists the program keeps her young. Another lady who was bent over with the pain and stiffness of arthritis, now walks upright and insists that the daily exercise and diet of Venus de Milo helps her. A four year old comes with her grandmother on her doctor's recommendation for exercise.

An overweight housewife came in crying, her husband had just left her for someone else and she had small children to raise. She is now slim, confident, and the owner of a very fashionable dress shop.

Care, love, encouragement, and hope; these are all as much a part of Venus de Milo as the diet and exercise.

Many of the salons have a sign up in the coffee klatch center that says "God Doesn't Make Junk". What we try to do is to help our ladies see themselves as they want to be; as they can be...to get a mental image of themselves secure, beautiful, happy, and comfortable with themselves...to see themselves with a Venus mirror...to see themselves as the woman in the Book of Proverbs "all together".


*Our Secret*

We have gone from nothing to millionaires in 10 years because we depend on God for everything. We will not willfully violate God's Word or knowingly sin in any way. I read the Bible every morning, first thing, and read it completely through 6 to 10 times per year. And each time through it is new, exciting and different. Love is the answer and never puts anyone down. We are active in our church and attend regularly. We are constantly in prayer. We set out to know Him, to be broken by Him, and be in complete submission to Him. Now, that doesn't mean I'm a "Molly Milquetoast" or a "Dolly Doormat", it just means I seek God's will in my life. I'm willing to be teachable and my priorities are in correct scriptural order; my God, my husband - I am his helpmate, we work together - and my family. We have dedicated our children to Him and implored God to help us raise them.

Step by step, we just grow closer to the Lord and step by step, closer to eternity.

## Sold Salons

After Yuma, Sussie and I opened 5 more salons. There was never any real time off. We worked together and we worked hard. I could never have done it without her help. Sussie has an official title in the corporation, but to me she is always "my beloved sister".

After seven years of long work days and no vacation, I got out of bed one morning and fell flat on my face. Jack said, "That's enough! You are selling out." We sold the original six, but had so many people interested in buying salons that we developed and sold another 27, then the government said it was time to franchise. This was the beginning of the rapid growth. We now have over 180 salons in our chain and open approximately 7 new salons every month. We are now in the process of expanding to the East Coast. We have 13 sales representatives, who all started at Venus as salon members. Most of the franchises are either owned and/or managed by former Venus de Milo "Fatties".

We choose our franchisees very carefully. I believe if we get the correct woman our salons will always be the very best. She is selected for her attitude, she must have a genuine liking for people and she should have lost weight at a Venus salon. This makes her a believer in our program and makes it easier for her to persuade a member to lose weight.

We have a special in-house training institute for all our owners and they are so well trained that many will recover their original investment in a very short time.

## A Private Prayer

I am no longer a self-driver and I never worry. When all

this began I could only make one trip per month to town to pay bills and shop because gas was 50 cents per gallon. Now I've learned to never limit God. He is not too small for anything. In early 1977 I secretly prayed to God for a Rolls Royce, 25 salons and to help women become more beautiful. I told no one. In late 1977 I had my Rolls Royce, in 1978 there were over 30 salons, and I believe the last part continues to be answered daily.

I've learned two very important things. Be careful what you pray for because you will get it, and be careful what you do, as your sins will find you out.

I find each day I grow more humble before the Lord as his blessings keep pouring out. I remember it took me 9 months to pay for my baby's crib. It gave me such joy to go down and be able to buy nice things for my first grandchild.

## Ownership - A Family Affair

Venus de Milo is not only a family business for us, as my sister Lucy Hammack also has several salons, but for most of our owners also. We have several mother-daughter partnerships and sisters also.

Our salons are owned by women and quite often their husbands work with them in keeping the books and in other areas outside of the salons themselves, as the salons are for women only. We employ on the average of 4 women per salon and all have the chance to work up to owning their own salon.

It is this line of ownership, desire for independence, and the need for self-fulfillment women of today have that has created a boom situation in what is supposed to be a recession.

## The Salon

In not having long-term contracts we give a woman

definite goals. Her three month program has realistic and definite goals and she is freed from the pressure of monthly payments. She feels good about herself and her membership. And every woman who follows the diet plan and does her exercises will lose weight. But Venus is more than reducing, it is also social. At our very first salon we served coffee or tea in china cups and saucers. Even today our salons are always equipped with a klatsch corner.

Venus is a chance for women to get together, break their daily routine, make friends and just chat. At the same time they do lose weight.

Many women are overweight and quite often will become unhappy, distraught and unhealthy. We have seen the improvement of health, appearance, and restoration of self esteem. Thin is a number one concern in women today. Fashions and society say to be beautiful you must be slender. Women feel this pressure. And even though we are a very educated nation, most women do not know how to diet. They want to rely on someone or something to help their willpower. Our gals are trained to motivate women to lose weight. There is a great deal of empathy between owners and members because they too have fought the battle of the bulge and won! The diet is doctor approved, high-protein, low-carbohydrate, and salt free. Sometimes, through dieting alone, the simple changes in eating habits can cause a major change in a woman's life style and our equipment is designed to firm the female body.

Venus salons have recently added aerobic exercises to music. We also have added equipment to aid cardiovascular health programs. The salons sell vitamins, cosmetics and leotards.

## For Continued Success

Each month there is a general meeting and training session for salon owners. New techniques, motivation studies, sales and marketing techniques, are all provided. All is designed to keep the salon owners motivated and successful. Most of all, success stories are shared, family styled closeness is enjoyed, and the glory is given to God.

*Formula For Success*

Turn it all over to God, keep Him first in your life. Keep your business neat, clean, decorated and motivated. Care about your clients and their needs. Give your best always. Follow the honesty and high morals laid out in God's Book of Rules. And remember the scripture that admonishes us to love one another as He first loved us.

This is not only the success for Venus de Milo, it is my success for life. To stay simply humble before the Lord, seeking His will in my life so that others will not see me, but will see Jesus Christ in me. He loved me enough to die on the cross for me. I love Him enough to follow in faith and tell others what He has done in my life.

The Enlightenment Amplifiers

DARLENE GOTH-NEUMAN
313 North Kenter Avenue
Los Angeles, California 90049
(213) 472-8342

## DARLENE GOTH-NEUMAN

Who's stealing your power?

Stationed throughout humanity are key people who have accumulated enough insight to answer that question.

As a master of psychology and a human behaviorist for many years, Darlene Goth-Neuman has developed a simple language and set of tools to understand, confront, and take charge of what she calls Not-I's, which she claims are at the root of conflict, low self-esteem, and even poverty and overweight.

Crediting life as her greatest teacher, her concepts with which to disarm the debilitating emotions of anger, guilt, fear and insecurity have made her a popular speaker for corporations, professional associations, and business groups nationwide. And her personal counseling schedule includes some of Hollywood's most elite.

She addresses herself to the topics of abundance, awareness, creative power, and weight loss with a charismatic graciousness marked by humor and a delightful honesty based on personal anecdote.

A resident director of the Los Angeles-based corporation, New Horizons, she is also the author of several books, including; "ABUNDANCE, HOW TO GET YOUR SHARE"; "THE KINGDOM OF THE NOT I'S"; and "AN AWARENESS APPROACH TO WEIGHT"; all of which, by unmasking the nature of the Not-I's, provide a unique process to eliminate stress and conflict from our daily lives.

# THE POWER OF THE NOT-I'S

### By Darlene Goth-Neuman

*"If I were a fatalist, or a mystic, which I decidedly am
not, it might be appropriate to say I believe in my lucky
star. But I reject "luck" - I feel every person creates his
own "determinism" by discovering his best aptitudes and
following them undeviatingly."*
### Walt Disney

I'd read every positive thinking book I could get my
hands on, attended church without fail, and had
relentlessly sought the elixir of truth in countless
philosophies, but I was in the depths of despair.

It was about a dozen years ago. Overweight, newly
divorced with five children to feed, I had no money and no
skills with which to earn a living. The church would leave
boxes of food and clothing on my back porch, which I was
far too embarrassed to admit even to my closest friend.

Despite a lifetime devoted to serving and pleasing
others, following Mother's advice to always do the right
thing, everything had gone wrong. Convinced I was a

failure, I simply gave up.

There's an old saying: "Nature abhors a vacuum." And so into the vacuum of life, happenstance dropped the first principles for taking charge of my thoughts and actions that was for me nothing short of miraculous.

How miraculous will wait, but for now let me just say what a shock it was to learn that my only true failing was searching for solutions to my problems in the first place! My approach to happiness turned topsy-turvy when I discovered that observing my inner state was the path to free me from the tyranny of my outer problems, and those very problems became valuable tools to illuminate my way.

## Power from Within

I'm sure you're already familiar with the notion, stated quite a few times in this book, that power or mastery of self comes from within. And it's true.

You also probably have friends, loved ones, and daily crises heaping demands upon you to the extent that the four harmful emotions of anger, guilt, fear, and insecurity create such turmoil that you're often powerless to cope.

Consequently, you may think, "If only this book can help me internalize what a wonderful human being I really am, then I can better explain to others how deserving I am of all the pleasure, comfort, attention, approval, and importance that I presently feel cheated of, but lack the confidence to express. And won't life be wonderful when I'm in control!"

But in control of whom?

The object of the preceding passage of thought is not mastery of self, but power over others to stop aggravating you. And that's where most readers of self-help books go wrong by unconsciously basing their expectations of happiness upon an outer ideal, usually another person, or occasionally on a thing or event.

Yet it's a simple fact of life that nobody's perfect.

So it should come as no great surprise that expectations dependent upon the manipulation of others are bound to explode in one's face. However, what frequently results is a wounded sense of indignation or disappointment. Then, whether vocalized or not, blame:

> They made me angry!
> She made me guilty!
> He made me afraid!
> You made me insecure!

Blame is power. And when power, which is itself neutral, is employed as harmful emotion it's then not free to be used creatively. So whenever you blame, no matter how right, proper, and justified you feel, you are giving your power away.

There are no victims, only unwitting volunteers.

So...how in heaven's name can you create and maintain a personal state of serenity when everybody's always pushing your buttons and your power is flying off every which way in reaction?

## The Master Decision

First, recognize that such harmful emotions are not an inherently natural part of you. Instead, it's the mischief of what, for simplicity's sake, I will call THE MASTER DECISION and the SIX NOT-I'S which since infancy have created an entrenched and unconscious MECHANICAL CONDITIONING within you based on CONFLICT.

And second, by exercising the tools by which you may DIS-IDENTIFY with the NOT-I'S through SELF OBSERVATION, WITHOUT JUDGEMENT OR CONDEMNATION, so that your REAL - I may surface and function FREE FROM CONFLICT.

Then and only then will you have gained the wisdom to exercise the power of choice in your life, to respond rather than react to challenge. There are no limitations to the power of a balanced and centered Real-I.

We conditioned human beings believe we have the power of choice until someone comes along and pushes the right buttons, whereupon we react mechanically and dump the responsibility of our actions on whatever upset us.

In reality, a conditioned person has no free will at all. (Ask any dieter!) The Not-I's are backstage running the show.

What are the Not-I's? They are servants of the Master Decision. But first, to explain the Master Decision we must go back to before the beginning.

From conception to birth the glimmering consciousness of a fetus becomes accustomed to the nondisturbed protection and nourishment of his mother's womb which cushions him from all manner of shocks and unpleasantries.

The newborn, however, faces a strange new world and soon arrives at the visceral conclusion that:

THE PURPOSE OF LIVING IS TO REGAIN
THE NONDISTURBED STATE BY GAINING
COMFORT AND PLEASURE AND ESCAPING
PAIN ON ALL LEVELS.

This is the Master Decision which shapes our lives from birth to death. It's born from four dual basic urges to:

GAIN COMFORT AND ESCAPE PAIN
GAIN ATTENTION AND ESCAPE REJECTION
GAIN APPROVAL AND ESCAPE DISAPPROVAL
GAIN IMPORTANCE AND ESCAPE INFERIOR-
ITY

Because we are unaware that this is our purpose of living, we are constantly subject to suggestions promising those things we want to gain and threatening those things we want to escape in the world around us. Our psyches become so literally cluttered with suggestions programming our lives, that our personal power is almost wholly spent running after the fulfillment of a host of desires which we unconsciously hope will lead us back to the nondisturbed state. But since a nondisturbed state can't be maintained by passing satisfactions, we wind up on an endless treadmill pursuing false ideals of more, better, and different.

Not-I's are created from infancy as servants of the Master Decision:

First: The baby cries. This gets all sorts of wonderful attention: food, cuddling, diapers changed. It's such a wonderful strategem that, as the child grows, he becomes very artful at what we term COMPLAINING.

Second: If crying doesn't get immediate results, the baby gets mad and cries louder, demanding to have his way right now in no uncertain terms. This generally speeds things up, and the baby becomes adept at DEFENDING his rights.

Third: Conflict is born when the toddler finally pushes too hard, and Mom and Dad lay down the law. Having temporarily exhausted the effectiveness of the first two methods, the toddler resorts to PLEASING in order to get his way. It's a compromise, but it works.

Fourth: Conflict grows inward as the child is exposed to outside influences and becomes aware of new ideas contrary to his own instincts offered by various authorities including his friends, and he finds it's often important that he BELIEVE and do as they say.

Fifth: Conflict becomes deeply suppressed as youth learns to PRETEND and act differently than he feels. As a social chameleon he is able to ease his way through the world by merely paying lip service to what he thinks is expected of him and get by.

Sixth: When all else fails and conflict hits the fan, he BLAMES. The blamer carries the burden of the world upon his shoulders, because if only things were different, life would improve. He beats his chest and rails against resistance, but seldom does anything about it.

## THESE ARE THE SIX NOT-I's:

| | |
|---|---|
| PRETENDER | BLAMER |
| PLEASER | DEFENDER |
| BELIEVER | COMPLAINER |

These tormenting little voices inside our heads sometimes referred to as conscience, are operative in our lives all the time. They batter contradictions back and forth, each in turn claiming to know what should have been or what ought to be. They seduce our thoughts into the past or future with such distractions as regret and resentment or hope and desire and, as a consequence, our personal power is lost when removed from the present. We can only creatively actualize in the now, not a second ago or two weeks from now. The present moment is all we have.

It's the Not-I's who rise to the occasion when our buttons are pushed, who fire harmful emotions associatively linked with the past or future. And the way they get away with it is, no one ever told us that these inner mischief-makers function as separate personalities other than our real selves. They are not you and they are not I.

The Real-I of a conditioned human being lies dormant, obscured by the deceit of the Not-I's like a beautiful butterfly not yet emerged from its cocoon.

In order to learn how to disidentify with the Not-I's, it's first necessary to consider the nature of resistance, and by resistance I mean anything that gets in your way. A clear definition is, "if you don't like it, it's resistance."

## Problems are Tools

Earlier when I said my problems became valuable tools in mastering self awareness, I was speaking of resistance. Resistance is a necessary force for development. Just as a muscle-builder deliberately exercises with weights to build his strength, so must we regard those people and circumstances who oppose us as opportunities to exercise self awareness.

Not-I's operate through feelings, and it is by observing our feelings at every waking moment that we can begin to strip them of their power. Resistance provides the magic mirror to illuminate them operating behind anger, guilt, fear and insecurity.

When you can recognize that it wasn't Aunt Martha's drinking problem which made you mad (or any other situation you can think of), but it was a Not-I within you reacting to Aunt Martha's drinking problem, then it suddenly becomes dazzlingly clear that Aunt Martha and her drinking problem no longer have the ability to wield power over you.

Thus, you're in charge, and the process of disowning the Not-I's has already begun, so bless Aunt Martha and all other resistance that comes your way, for without it you could not evolve.

During self-observation, the process just demonstrated of how to reclaim your power from the Not-I's by disidentifying with them, you may discover a few disagreeable chinks in your self image. However, it's important to observe Not-I's objectively without judgement or condemnation because it halts the process. Be kind to yourself.

And be patient. At first you'll find self observation usually follows with a time lag after whatever resistance you encounter. But with perseverance, you'll begin to see your feelings unfold as though watching a home movie.

As you continue to observe and disidentify with the

Not-I's, pretty soon you're likely to experience surprise that you no longer react to certain things in the mechanically conditioned way you used to, not by suppressing emotion, but by having allowed your Real-I a chance to grow where the Not-I's once flourished.

When this happens, you're suddenly capable of responding to life spontaneously and creatively. And that's power. Real and Awake living beings create their own world.

## Opportunity From Humiliation

So what happened to the poor, fat divorcee with five mouths to feed? Well, you may recall that one of the humiliations of my life was my dependence on the boxes of food and clothing the church would leave on my back porch.

My family never had enough money for new clothes, but since I was too proud to ever let anyone, even my best friend, know we were that poor, out of clever desperation I'd always taken my needle and thread to the old hand-me-downs and reworked them into neat, fashionable apparel for myself and the children. And nobody ever suspected.

Now, forced by circumstances of the divorce to take charge, it dawned on me that thrift shops specializing in tasteful second-hands were booming. I gave my best friend the shock of her life when I blurted out the truth about how I managed to dress the family, and we went into business together.

We worked day and night. I did the buying, selling, and decorating, and she did the bookkeeping. Our elegant little shop, frequented by doctors' and lawyers' wives and celebrities, succeeded beyond our wildest dreams! She bought me out, and I made enough money to put myself through college in order to earn a masters degree in psychology. And all the while I worked with these principles, clearing out harmful emotions and worn out associations which kept surfacing like pickles in a barrel.

Yet for years I resisted the responsibility of sharing the principles with others. But my teacher, Robert Gibson, to whom I'll be eternally grateful, encouraged me to do so. And now I consider it a privilege to devote my life to shedding light on the misery of the Not-I's.

I now spend much of my time conducting seminars on corporate sales motivation, as well as intensive workshops on abundance and prosperity, weight loss (without diets), and self-awareness. In addition, I hold private consultations with people from all walks of life including top executives and celebrities. The aim of all this is to provide people with tools for self understanding which enables them to live without conflict. And it works!

## Free the Real-I

Over the years I've worked with thousands of people and have delighted in watching their Real-I's expand to include spiritual power, material abundance, and fulfilling relationships in their lives as a result of freeing themselves to experience life fully. There are no limitations to the power of a balanced and centered Real-I.

Having advanced from a despairing divorcee to the resident director of a Los Angeles-based corporation, a now-slender me, can confidently walk into any Beverly Hills designer boutique and pick anything off the racks without the slightest regard to price tags. Sound pretentious? It isn't, it's fun! Life is a celebration when the Not-I's no longer have power over you. Take it from me, I know.

Socrates said, "Know thyself," and truly therein lies the source of real personal power.

*"Tis the mind that makes the body rich."*
*William Shakespeare*

The Enlightenment Amplifiers

RON USELDINGER, M.A.
National Director
Fitness Motivation Institute of America
36 Harold Avenue
San Jose, California 95117
(408) 246-9191

## RONALD E. USELDINGER, M.A.

Ron Useldinger is one of the nation's most sought after convention speakers. He has traveled over one million miles evangelizing the positive benefits of being physically fit. His new book "ISOROBICS - A Better Way to Fitness" has been a big success. He has also written articles for national magazines and has appeared on many leading TV talk shows throughout the country. Ron has a Masters Degree in Physical Education, and is, himself, an award winning high school and college athlete. A dynamic motivator as a coach, his high school teams in football and wrestling won several major championships in California. He is a member of the American Association of Fitness Directors in Business and Industry, has served on the AAU Council on Physical Fitness and the American and California Associations of Health, Physical Education and Recreation. In addition, he is a CSP member of the National Speakers Association and is listed in Who's Who in Business and Industry in America. He also serves as the National Director of his own company, Fitness Motivation Institute of America, and as conditioning consultant for many of the top professional sports teams, including the Seattle Seahawks and the Golden State Warriors. He has produced five half-hour TV specials on physical fitness that are shown throughout the United States.

# THE POWER OF PHYSICAL FITNESS

*By Ron Useldinger*

*"Do you not know that your body is a temple of the Holy Spirit within you...So glorify God in your body."*
*I Cor. 6:19, 20*

My face to face encounter with my own mortality was not a dramatic event like a terrible automobile accident or diagnosis of a terminal illness. My brush with death at 30 years of age was an internal process which occurred on New Year's Day. I looked at myself in the mirror and didn't like what I saw. From a healthy football player of 185 pounds, I had allowed my weight to slowly creep up to a flabby 215 pounds. I was out of shape and really out of control. My manly figure of broad shoulders and narrow waist had reversed itself.

While I stared at myself in the bathroom mirror, I knew that what I was doing to my body was going to hasten my death. I was tired at noon and asleep in front of the television by eight in the evening. I didn't like what I saw, I was deeply unhappy.

I was out of the habit of physical exercise. I knew that to really take proper care of my body I had to get into a pattern as automatic as brushing my teeth and combing my hair.

Before I even began to consider what I might do to improve the terrible state into which my body had fallen, I knew all the drawbacks of exercise. I knew the boredom. I knew the fatigue and soreness. I knew how many people died on the first few days of the year as they suddenly attempted to reform their lives in an unrealistic resolve to make up, in a matter of days, what years of overeating and underexercising had caused.

## *Me, The High School Football Coach*

That New Year's Day, I really took stock of the direction my life was headed. My priorities were God, family and work. Physical fitness wasn't even in the running! What made this so ironic was that I was employed as a high school football coach and really loved what I was doing. I had no trouble getting kids out on the field to work very hard two hours a day, week after week. Yet I did not take the time for myself. The hypocrisy of my body saying one thing while I mouthed another was suddenly too apparent to me. I was ashamed.

My mind reasoned over the problem. I had always thought I was a great motivator but maybe I wasn't. For the first time, it occurred to me that a person has to be self-motivated. Another person can attempt to inspire us but there is no real action unless it comes from within. Those students didn't get out on the field day after day just because of my pep talks, they got out there because they enjoyed the game. If the season wasn't scheduled with challenges from rival football teams, I knew that within a couple of weeks there would be no one out on the field.

But I had no real motivation to change my ways. I was disgusted with the way I looked and felt. Even the prospect of losing my family and work prematurely, due to my excess fat and hardened arteries, didn't make me move.

*Five Factors that Create Problems*

1. TIME. One of the key problems for anyone like myself, who suddenly realizes he needs to change, is the problem of TIME. I'm not the only one who feels there are never enough hours in a day. Even my job as high school football coach was not providing the vigorous exercise that my body needed. I knew it was foolhardy to attempt to fit into the weekends what I wasn't doing daily. Just as the first few days of January score an inordinate amount of fatal heart attacks for those who abruptly launch into something their bodies are ill-prepared for, the sharp rise of heart attacks on Saturdays and Sundays underlines a similar phenomena. It seemed impossible for me to allocate sufficient time on a daily basis. I wished for something that could be as automatic for me as shaving. But the habit was not there. Shaving took a lot less time than any exercise program I had ever heard of.

2. BOREDOM. Another prominent setback to my plans for an exercise program is the repetition which is intrisically boring. We must keep increasing the number of any particular exercise to reap the same positive gains. For example, if I do five push-ups today, a year from now I must do 105 to reap the same benefits. Nothing good in terms of improvement or change takes place until the person exercising begins to tire. Cumulative buildup of exercises are necessary. But more and more repetition of the same exercise spells boredom.

3. SORENESS. Another major problem in exercise is

SORENESS. Nobody had to tell me how stiff and sore one can get when a rigorous reform program is attempted. I have gotten out of bed after a few days of overdoing and exclaimed, "I'm in pain. That's it. No more. I quit." What happened was a buildup of lactic acid which is a simple by-product of a working muscle.

Another type of soreness is the actual physical injuries that I could inflict on myself by an activity like jogging. I was already overweight. My extra weight would serve to add extra impact every time my foot hit the sidewalk. I would send a tremendous jolt to my ankles, knees, hips and lower back on every bounce. With every stride my weight was amplified from over 200 pounds to a staggering 600 pounds!

4. INCONVENIENCE. We live in a world where sitting fourteen hours a day is common. Getting the right exercise is downright INCONVENIENT. I knew all the reasons why it would be inconvenient for me. I didn't want to "suit up" and go out there and face the neighbors. If I attempted to jog, I was sure I would be chased by every dog in the neighborhood. I thought nobody could see my problem. I wanted to keep my resolution to reform a secret. Wasn't there something I could do in the privacy of my own home? Maybe even in the closet?

I know for others there is also the problem of thinking of exercise in the form of a competitive sport. This idea really adds to the inconvenience! If you have to reserve a court and line up a partner for racquetball or tennis, it is much easier to procrastinate. Not everybody likes competitive sports either.

So when I confronted myself on that January morning I had a new insight into MOTIVATION because of my own personal lack of it. I realized that instead of motivation coming from somebody else, MOTIVATION MUST COME FROM WITHIN. Every person has to find his or her own reason to exercise. My own reason was the recognition of what I would lose so soon if I did not get the regular healthful exercise my body desperately needed. I wanted to look good, feel good and be physically fit.

5. ENLIGHTENMENT. That month of January was difficult for me. I knew the problem but I didn't have a viable solution. I knew all the reasons why the conventional resolutions that most people make wouldn't work for me. I didn't have the "easy out" of fooling myself. I knew as a coach that easy solutions were unrealistic.

Fortunately, I was scheduled to attend a football clinic in Palo Alto at the end of January. Attending such a clinic is a rather standard activity for a football coach, so I did not enter that room with any expectation that what I would hear would be any more than coaching advice. Three hours later I came out a changed man. I had a solution to my problem from a most unexpected source. You could even say the answer came to me from outer space!

At that particular clinic, scientists who worked for N.A.S.A. came and shared with us a small simple piece of equipment which the astronauts were using to exercise in our country's space program. As I watched the device being demonstrated, I was awestruck by the simple wisdom of the concept.

*The Isorobic Exercise System*

The piece of equipment these scientists designed for the astronauts use weighed less than two pounds, yet it rivaled the versatility of a gymnasium full of exercise equipment. When I had contemplated the idea of being a "closet exerciser" I had never considered the confined space in which astronauts must exercise to keep their bodies in optimum condition!

By adjusting a small dial, the demonstrators of the

ISOROBIC UNIT controlled the amount of resistance and speed with which the device could be used. I immediately recognized the value of this feature. I was greatly impressed with the comprehensiveness with which this device could be used to meet the variety of different exercise needs of our bodies.

The proper use of the Isorobic exercise unit combined the best features of Isometrics, Isotonics, Isokinetics and Aerobic Exercise. To explain why each of these are essential to us, I will call a little "time out" right here to explain these principles.

An ISOMETRIC exercise is a static contraction of the muscle. You can pull or push while tightening your muscle, thus building up strength very quickly. Ten seconds is the optimal time for benefitting from this exercise. When Isometrics became the rage, the average American got a little too carried away with the simplicity of it all. He would say, "Hey, here's the answer to my problem. All I'm going to have to do is get up every morning tighten every muscle in my body for ten seconds, run over, take a shower and I'm done." This sounded great, but unfortunately it doesn't work out that way. While it is true that you can build up strength in such a fashion, you are doing nothing for your heart, lungs, and arteries. Isometric exercise does not help flexibility or muscle balance. It only builds up brute strength in the particular area in which it is being used.

ISOTONIC exercise means exercise with movement. One of the objectives of exercise with movement is fatigue which is possible with repetitive isotonic exercise. Fatigue can be hastened with the use of weights. When I was in high school, the coach always warned us against the use of weights. "You'll be able to lift barbells and not be able to scratch the back of your neck", he advised us. Certainly this is an exaggeration but it does underline the difficulty connected with leverage. It takes more strength to get things moving than to keep them moving. The value of the weight lifting changes dramatically according to the leverage or angle from gravity in which we position our bodies.

ISOKENETIC exercise allows for the variations in our leverage angle by controlling resistance and speed. This allows for complete exercise of the muscles rather than just those called into play in traditional weight lifting exercises. The muscle works consistently through the entire range of motion. Nowadays, major gymnasiums have very expensive equipment to allow members this maximum advantage of their exercise efforts.

AEROBICS is the form of exercise that is now very popular. Basically, it is fast activity, sometimes dancing, which causes the heart, lungs and arteries to work hard. Aerobics stimulates the heart rate and heart pressure. The goal is working until the rate of heart beat has been raised sufficiently to create a conditioning effect on the heart muscle.

For a person to be totally fit, he or she must have all these forms of exercise. It is not enough for a person to look fit. Recently a man who had just won one of those "body-beautiful contests" failed the Seattle police examination because he could not get on and off a chair for three minutes. Everyone knows stories of people who have just walked out from a medical examination where they were pronounced in the best of health only to drop dead of a heart attack.

## Three Days and Seventy-Nine Orders

By the conclusion of the Isorobic exercise system demonstration at the football clinic, I had become a true believer. I saw that the advantages of this device went far beyond just my team's performance or my own well-being. I couldn't wait to get back to school and demonstrate it for my football players. I showed it to everybody and anybody. This marvelous little device, weighing less than two pounds, integrated the best qualities of ISOMETRICS, ISOTONICS, ISOKINETICS and AEROBICS!

I, who was once so reluctant to even admit to myself that I had a problem, was now shouting to the world that I had an answer! Within three days, I had seventy-nine orders for the Isorobic Exercise System and I wasn't even selling them! Imagine the surprise of the demonstrators when I showed up on their doorstep. I was immediately invited to work as a consultant with the designers of the unit who used it with the Apollo Space Program.

What was so appealing to me is that I could use the system for only six to fifteen minutes a day and get a total workout. This certainly was the solution I had been desperately looking for. I soon realized I had reprioritized my life. Happiness to me is God first, health, family and job. Without health, none of us would be able to have family or job for very long.

## Helping Others

My discovery of the ISOROBIC EXERCISE SYSTEM expanded my horizons. Before, my interest was basically just helping my players and students. After that one football clinic, I was interested in everybody's fitness.

My involvement as a consultant opened many new doors. I found it a real honor to participate in research for our space program. We found out important factors related to inactivity and were able to take measures to prevent these stresses from occurring in the cramped confines of the space capsule. I have now worked with a wide range of famous athletes, football players, basketball players, hockey players, and runners. I have had the pleasure of observing their remarkable advances in strength and flexibility through the use of the ISOROBIC EXERCISE UNIT. My greatest satisfaction probably comes from helping average individuals whose own situations are similar to the one that I confronted when I faced my mirror that fateful New Year's Day so long ago.

I now weigh 183 pounds and can do things far superior to what I could do at the age of 25; this includes running a six-minute mile! I am happier than I ever was before, because now I realize how fitness and happiness go hand in hand. I tour the country telling people they will be happy when they look good, feel good and are physically fit. I serve as a living example of the positive power of physical fitness and how to achieve it.

*"Ignorant people raise questions that wise ones answered a thousand years ago."*

The Enlightenment Amplifiers

CAROLINE TICEN
Masters Associates
4473 Caminito Pedernal
San Diego, California 92117
(714) 272-8497

## CAROLINE TICEN

Caroline was an invalid with Multiple Sclerosis until she got in touch with self-healing and personal power. Through a series of processes she was able to experience miraculous healing after years of illness.

Caroline is rapidly emerging at the forefront to be one of the newest, dynamic, motivational speakers in the country. When Caroline talks to people, a powerful kind of energy develops. The barriers disappear as each person gets in touch with their own power to create magic and miracles in their own life. Caroline not only speaks and motivates, but entertains as well. She is a professional singer and loves to incorporate music into her programs.

Caroline reveals the principles of healing in her speeches and seminars. The principles of healing work miracles in all areas of life, whether in business, sales relationships, health or self-esteem. Since experiencing her own miracle, Caroline created and is co-owner of the Magic and Miracles Factory which produces Magic Wands. The Magic Wand is a gift item sold in boutiques and gift stores nationwide. It consists of a white porcelain star with a rainbow painted on it. It is also available with a unicorn. The star is attached to a wooden dowel and ribbon streamers and a special story is tied on. It is completely handmade.

Caroline is also on the staff of APPLAUSE MAGAZINE in San Diego. It is the program magazine for the Opera, Symphony, and all performing arts events.

The most advanced, unique learning technology is used in the cassette tapes Caroline produces. She has studied Superlearning, Right Brain - Left Brain, Alpha and Theta

Programming which are incorporated into self-healing, meditations and stress reduction.

Programs vary from one hour keynote addresses to full day workshops. Special programs will be created just for your personal needs. Some of Caroline's presentations include: Guided Learning Through Meditation, Management Effectiveness, Personal Effectiveness, Stress Reduction, Total Aliveness, Personal Power, The Magic's In Me.

A speaking engagement with Caroline is a delightful blend of inspiration and entertainment.

Caroline is putting together a radio show featuring Holistic Health and Healing. She wants to give those who are ill the courage to live an unlimited life. Caroline's personal philosophy is that peace, joy and ecstacy can only be attained with Mastery of life and right living.

*"Man was made in the image of God." I do not believe that this refers to the physical image but to the soul or spirit or mind. Every one of us was entrusted at birth with a precious fragment of the Divine Mind to develop for good or evil. That we may know how to develop it for good, God in His infinite wisdom gave us the pattern whereby we can keep alive this precious birthright - the Divine spark within us. This pattern He gave us is the Ten Commandments.*

*Cecil B. DeMille*

# 8

### POSITIVE POWER PEOPLE
*The Enlightenment Amplifiers*

# THE MAGIC POWER'S IN ME

*By Caroline Ticen*

*"The magic and power of hope upon human exertion and happiness is wonderful. Always bear in mind that your own resolution to succeed is more important than any other one thing."*

*Abraham Lincoln*

A miracle is nothing more than an ordinary person doing extraordinary things.

"Ladies and Gentlemen, the woman you are about to meet has a most unique story to tell. She has come from the depths of an incurable disease to be a successful speaker, inspiring and motivating all who hear her. She is also the creator and owner of a manufacturing plant that produces Magic Wands which are sold nationwide...."

I listened to his words of praise as I stood near the platform waiting to speak to hundreds of people. I, who only a few years ago, didn't have the courage or strength to speak to one individual, much less a whole crowd. I came from a generation where children were seen and not heard, where it wasn't acceptable to express emotions or show anger. Women and children were sheltered and kept in their place. I learned what many of us learn; that we're not OK the way we are, not quite capable, not quite lovable. We find a way to cope and survive. I created dis-ease. The doctor had told me three years before I had an incurable disease. His sentence was clear and cruel: "Life's imprisonment - no parole, no pardon, no hope."

At that time I was staggered as much by the identity of the sentencer as by his words. My doctor, my physician, counselor, and friend, had condemned me to endless captivity - without trial and without my ever having committed a crime.

My prison would be my own paralyzed body. My jailer, Multiple Sclerosis. I remember the overpowering fear that numbed me when he said in a practiced, professionally detached way, "Sorry, Caroline, there's no cure. There is just no cure."

I did not know then that the prison was truly of my own making. I had created it myself, over the years, by closing psychological doors, by gradually walling-off parts of me to gnaw secretly at my very being.

## I Accepted My Role

For the previous thirteen years I had been the perfect minister's wife. I accepted my role and played it to perfection. Always dependable, I went to all the church meetings and sat on committees. I stood behind my husband, always careful to be submissive and not usurp his limelight. There was no love or respect, a mere facade of a marriage.

We had stayed together all those years simply because we didn't know what else to do. The consequences of divorcing a minister was too painful to consider.

He was doing what he had trained and studied for. He was living out his dream. And I was doing what he thought I ought to do. Yet I had unfulfilled dreams of a life with love and joy. I wanted to be appreciated. I wanted to make a contribution with my life. And all the while I smiled and nodded politely with deep resentment and resignation.

It was in those days that the first tiny signs of my illness started: the fatigue, the occasional numbness in my arms and legs. I barely noticed them then. To an unhappy woman, the sleep that follows fatigue is a welcome refuge.

Every day the bright spots in my life grew dimmer. At last there was no light anywhere and I knew I could not go on. I saw three choices: to kill myself, to have a mental breakdown, or to leave.

I chose what I now know was the most difficult. I left. And in so doing, I closed the door on suppressed guilt and fear.

To leave a husband is bad enough. To leave your children was considered unforgivable. I love my children with the fervor and passion of a devoted mother, yet I had to leave my two sons behind. My physical and emotional state was deteriorating and I knew that to care for both boys and their sister would push me over the edge. I had no education, no recent job experience, and no money to hire babysitters. I made the decision in a conscious way, knowing it was ultimately the best for us all. I found that my gifts of my spirit, love, honesty and understanding have helped them to be stronger and better people. We have a bond of love and respect that is very special.

I remember the guilt I felt as I waved good-by to my confused, red-eyed little boys. I couldn't endure that guilt and locked it away deep inside.

In the years that followed I thought I had dealt with the guilt and was done with it. But I hadn't, and it wasn't done with me. While I played the new role of single career-woman, that guilt, like the resentment of the years before, ate away at my nerves to bring the days of my imprisonment inexorably closer.

## *The Illusion of Romance*

The ex-minister's wife led a fabulous life. I went to glamorous places and met glamorous people. The most glamorous of all was Bill, with whom I fell instantly, helplessly in love.

He was handsome, worldly, romantic. He stirred feelings of womanhood I never knew I had. We loved adventure. We traveled, we ate and drank, we danced ourselves to exhaustion. We lived in a world of fantasy. Too quickly, we got married.

Spurred on by new intensity, I began selling life insurance. It was a way to make a great deal of money and prove myself. I had to know I could make it in a difficult, demanding business.

I did well, motivated not only out of desire for greatness, but out of fear of failure. The pace of my life quickened. Every day I went from the fantasy of my life with Bill to the even more intense hard-driving world of sales and back again. My dual passions were consuming. I had no time for introspection and spiritual growth. I could only continue.

The fatigue and pain got worse. It became part of my life, while I told myself I was just tired from a full day's work. When I began to complain and compensate for my symptoms, Bill refused to understand. His fantasy-world didn't include a sick wife. He wanted only the unencumbered, unspoiled fairy tale. Our differences became irreconcilable. I then found myself locking another door. Again I left, feeling unloved and unappreciated.

After leaving Bill I submerged in a mindless round of furious work and pleasure, interrupted only by ever lengthening bouts of pain and numbness.

I was determined to squeeze the most I could out of life. The more I experienced, the more I wanted and the more I wanted, the less satisfaction I got. I threw myself into my work. I sold lots of insurance, got lots of pats on the back, and began feeling good about my success, though not about myself.

I jammed my life full of business appointments, dates, and outings with my children. What I didn't know was that I was shutting away my feelings of inadequacy. What I didn't know was that I was advancing myself to a severe stage of Multiple Sclerosis.

My left leg was almost constantly numb. I seemed to hurt all over, but especially in my chest and back. At first, the doctors said there was nothing wrong.

Eventually, I went into the hospital. After tests, specialists, conferences, and more tests, Dr. Swank was able to pronounce sentence; I had an incurable disease, Multiple Sclerosis.

### Sentenced to Maximum Security Prison

After the fear subsided it was replaced by rage, then a helpless, hopeless sorrow. But then something strange began to happen. I felt almost relieved - as if a giant burden was being lifted from me.

The pain was still there, of course, but it was almost like an irritable old friend, one whom you tolerate because of familiarity. I had lived with it for a long time, and now, in some curious way, I began to find my situation comfortable.

Having worked for an insurance company, I had a fantastic set of policies: hospitalization, major medical, disability income, the works. I was an invalid with no worries or responsibilities. Financially secure and with my illness to buffer any demands that could be made of me, I was totally safe. I had built myself a prison of maximum-security kind. I had constructed it to protect me from the world.

My life seemed to consist only of pain and pills. The pain grew to be almost constant. I drifted in consciousness from the delirium of drug-induced sleep.

To say now that I enjoyed that life sounds very strange. But as bleak as it was, it seemed the only alternative to the "normal" life that had made me a mental and spiritual invalid. By comparison the life of a physical invalid was an easy one.

A friend moved in, cooked, cleaned and lovingly cared for me. When my daughter had to leave me and live with her father, it was as if everything I had ever owned, loved, cherished, or wanted was now taken away from me. I became fiercely angry at myself, my fate, the people around me, the very world in which I was living.

Anger with nowhere to go is soon replaced by self-pity. Poor me! Self-pity tugged at me and sapped my remaining strength.

Fortunately, rather than trying to think - to analyze, rationalize, or justify - I then began to meditate, to look within at my spiritual self. Meditation revealed to me that although I had been deprived of everything, I still had one valuable treasure left. TIME.

I had time to stop, to get off the roller-coaster, time to discover what my life really was, what I, myself, really was. I had time to discover that what I thought was God's punishment was actually grace and opportunity for growth.

*Truth is Power*

When I opened myself up and surrendered to my

spiritual growth, I soon connected with others who were committed to their spiritual journey. The major influence in my spiritual understanding has been a group called Subud. Subud essentially means Right Living manifested in your life through surrender and worship to God.

Meditation helped me to begin to see clearly, I viewed my life as a gigantic puzzle. I saw each person, each experience, each period of my life as a piece of a puzzle, and each piece represented a lesson I had set out to learn in life. As the whole came into focus I came to a staggering - almost devastating - realization: I had created it all myself.

I saw that I had been allowing people to manipulate me all my life.

I saw that what I had been interpreting as resentment of others for degrading me was actually my resentment of myself. All the destructive feelings I had locked inside were my own destructive feelings toward myself. No one had "done it" to me. I was my own persecutor. Because of an unconscious decision that I was not worthwhile, not an equal of others, not an adequate person, I had spent my life degrading myself!

I realized that whatever power I had possessed, I mentally gave away. I had abdicated the throne of my own majestic being. I had flung the staff of power from my own hands by telling one basic, gigantic lie: that I was inferior.

With that immense realization there came a second, more profound awareness: Truth is power. I saw that the truth actually does make us free. I knew for the first time that the way out of my prison was through the simple act of telling the truth and living the truth. My friends supported me in my quest to be assertive and tell the truth. When I told them my feelings, there was instant communication and we got to the heart of the problem. However, if I carried anger around, barriers went up. The longer I waited, the higher they got.

I started seeing small miracles happening in my relationships in the way people treated me. I demanded respect and I got it. I demanded honesty and I got it. I decided not to be at the effect of anyone or anything again. I realized with a sudden knowingness that I had the power to heal myself through God's love.

My whole life had been a struggle, filled with strife, trouble: a death process. I had accepted pain as a way of life, pain in relationships and now pain in my body. The thought occurred to me that healing would take place when I no longer saw any value in pain. Was the pain serving me? It had kept people and relationships away from me. It had kept the love that I truly wanted away from me. All of a sudden I saw that my sickness was a decision. I had decided on weakness rather than strength. I also realized that there was a paradox here, for to have real strength, I had to be strong in a different way. I had to be open and vulnerable, willing to expose myself. I decided that I wanted to be responsible for my life. I wanted to be healed.

This knowledge was terribly frightening. It meant that there would be no more excuses. My mind suddenly sprang back into battle with my spirit.

"Don't give up the disease!" it argued. "Look what a great situation you've got here. It's nice and safe. Everyone takes care of you."

"How long do you think you can last in the world with all the stress and pressure? Look how relaxed you are now. You'll never be able to relax like that again if you get well."

My spirit, on the other hand, spoke with confidence. It said, "Yes, being well will be difficult. But it's the only way you'll ever experience who you really are. It's the only way you'll ever be able to make a difference in this world."

My spirit said that I must release the things which served only to hold me down - the pain which fed upon my guilt; the disease which kept me from participating in the life I feared. Most of all I had to release the need to be safe.

I was seized by the need to put my awareness into action. My friends packed me up and moved me all the way to a small town in Arizona.

By this time, I was better. I was able to get around, but still had many symptoms and much pain.

My new friends in Arizona taught me "creative visualization." In my inner eye I began to see myself running and jumping joyfully, tirelessly, in a lush, green meadow dotted with white daisies and blue lupin. I saw myself as physically beautiful again, and I floated through the high grass like an antelope on strong, healthy legs. I began to view my sickly body as something apart from the real "me". I thought of it as "over there," coping with its symptoms. I began to let go of pain, guilt, and disease.

I went to a spiritual retreat in Monterey and there were many seminars, but much time for meditation, also. One afternoon, I sat at the ocean feeling the moist spray on my face and the sun and breeze dancing around me, teasing me to stay there forever. I became very quiet. There unfolded before me the chapters of my life and all the people I had lived with in varying degrees of love, hate, hurt and need.

*Healing is Forgiveness*

As each person appeared, we went into the "inner room of my heart" where there was only light of love and forgiveness.

The first person to come in with me was my mother whom I have loved so dearly but not always had good communications with. Events happened through the years and out of them grew ill feelings and barriers. First, I told her all the expectations I had about her that had not been fulfilled. She listened to me, her eyes sad and often filling with tears, and I could see that she felt inadequate and unfulfilled too. I also expressed all the things I wished I would have done with her. I thanked her for all the care and love she had given to me as I was growing up. She wept and I wept. She replied softly, "Yes, there are so many things I wish I had taken the time to do with you. My life has not turned out as I dreamed it would. I guess I just got wrapped up in my own problems." I replied, "I know, Mother. I know you loved me all that you could and gave me all that you could give to me. You did your very best. I forgive you and please forgive me too." We looked at each other with a pure, unconditional love. And I forgave myself.

She was followed by my father, my children, my former husbands, then friends and people whom I had not thought about for years. One by one, I met them, came to terms with them, and released them. One by one, they told me they loved me and disappeared. I cried the deep sweet-tasting tears of someone experiencing not sorrow, but released anger, pain and God's forgiveness.

As I cried I began to feel light - so light that I wondered if I still had a body. With the anticipation of health, the fear returned for a brief second. I dispelled it instantly with these words: "From this moment on, I totally surrender. I choose life and not death."

As I clearly saw my spirit, I perceived what I can only call God. A powerful force of brilliant, healing purple light shone and shimmered before me.

Then the light began whirling and I saw and felt it enter the crown of my head, moving through my body, touching and healing every cell, every damaged nerve, every withered muscle. It moved down and then out with a terrific whooosh, a sound at the same time both deafening and soothing.

Instantly, I felt cleansed and pure. Instantly, I knew that healing is very simple. Healing and atonement are identical. To forgive is to heal.

I realized that in forgiving we return everything to a natural condition of oneness. At the moment of forgiveness I experienced a total unity of body, mind and spirit. At that moment my maximum-security prison was no more. At that moment I was healed.

I knew that I had to keep opening doors by telling the truth, asking for what I want and fulfilling my dreams. I knew the most important thing for me to do was to be all that I could be and let nothing hold me back. I knew that I had a magnificent purpose in this life. It was going to take a complete surrender of my mind, body and spirit to God's will for me. My life would take on meaning and ever be filled with joy and ecstacy.

And so, as if I had never heard of such a thing as disease, I leapt to my feet and walked - without pain or fear or guilt - to share a miracle with the world.

And as I walk on stage to address my audience, "I have brought you a Magic Wand to help you remember that you all have the power to create miracles in your life. We have forgotten how to use our power. We are all looking for a Genie, an Angel, or a Magic Wand to DO IT FOR US. But you see, the Magic's in you and the Magic's in me.

*"May you live all the days of your life."*
*Swift*

*"Light-Life. The prime work of God"*
*Milton [The Blind Poet]*

The Enlightenment Amplifiers

**BOB SWEENEY**
Olympic Figure and Fitness Clubs
Broadway House, Waterhouse Street
Halifax, West Yorkshire, England.
HALIFAX 58669

## BOB SWEENEY

Bob Sweeney from Halifax, England warns people that they may not survive their success unless they pay more than lip service to staying healthy. He has not only made a successful business, he has made Health his business. Starting with just $200, he has built a highly successful chain of health clubs in Great Britain. He has achieved many of the 'good things in life' along with Dynamic good health. After building his health and physique from his hobby of physical culture, which enabled him to become a successful professional wrestler, he developed his business and his education by an intensive self-improvement program which brought him to the United States several times to attend seminars. He is a member of the National Speakers Association and loves to help develop people further by teaching success principles via a 'Richer More Successful Life Course', 'Management and Motivation', and 'Stepping Stones in Selling'.

POSITIVE
POWER
PEOPLE
*The Enlightenment Amplifiers*

# HOW TO BE HEALTHY WEALTHY AND WISE

*By Bob Sweeney*

*"Men love to wonder, and that is the seed of our science."*
*Emerson*

## Simple Truths

Simple truths make up my philosophy to guarantee a life full of health, wealth and wisdom - a Super Life that is within the grasp of every man and woman. I came upon some of these truths by having the good fortune to be a keen reader of books and magazines.

I became enlightened by some of these simple truths after starting body building when I was about 17 years of age. Joe Weider, publisher of the world's greatest body building and fitness magazines, instilled in me through his writings that 'YOU COULD ACHIEVE ANYTHING YOU WANTED IF YOU BELIEVED IT WAS POSSIBLE AND WANTED IT STRONGLY ENOUGH'.

Through my own training and talking to champion bodybuilders I learned another simple truth, - that to build one's body required DISCIPLINE AND PATIENCE.

I found since then, by applying these same principles to other goals in my life, that indeed they are simple truths which will guarantee you all the good things in life - Health, Wealth, Knowledge, Peace of Mind, Security, Happiness, and Love. I guess most people would go along with that little list as requirements for a Super Life.

Many people who would like most of these things are 'wishing' their way through life because they don't accept simple truths such as BELIEF, DISCIPLINE, AND PATIENCE. They think there has to be some other secret, some easier way. Often they want everything today and end up with empty tomorrows.

I am still picking up more and more simple truths from two simple sources that are open to everyone, and that can enlighten your way to a Super Life.


*The Sources*

My first source is the Bible. After years of knocking it without ever reading it, I was encouraged to read it by one of the worlds most inspirational speakers and authors, a very successful business man and a wonderful human being, Zig Ziglar.

I found the Bible, that I had never read, full of

principles that made so much sense and when they were put to work, proved themselves to be true. Regardless of anyone's individual belief who could ever dispute such simple truths as, 'What you sow you reap'.

My second source is from successful people.

Contrary to what I used to think, successful people are generally the most willing people in the world to share their beliefs and principles of success. They love to tell you how they made it. You just need to have the courage to simply ask them, pick an appropriate time, of course, and give some appreciation to their time, but certainly find the time and the courage to talk to them. You'll be surprised at what you learn - you see most of them believe in another simple truth, 'YOU HAVE TO GIVE IN ORDER TO RECEIVE'. 'WHAT YOU GIVE OUT YOU GET BACK' - and often twenty fold or more.

Successful people often give lectures, write books and make cassette tapes. Devour them at every opportunity, look and listen for the simple truths and when you come across them believe them. By mixing with successful people who are willing to share their knowledge you'll find all kinds of opportunity thoughts evolving in your life.

There's just one type of person to avoid, and the advice they give. That's the person who tells you that in order to get on in life you have to be ruthless, that you have to trample on, and take advantage of people, that you need to cheat and to lie, that you just need to look out for yourself.

Some of these people write books based on these kind of morals and sometimes their techniques appear to work. My experience has been that they seldom stay successful, in whatever they are doing, and even if their business or financial state seems good they invariably foul up some other area of their life, such as their marriage or their health - the man or woman who has a million dollars in the bank and a stomach full of ulcers is certainly not living the super successful life that we are talking about.

Zig Ziglar wrote a magnificent book, SEE YOU AT THE TOP, and in it he introduced me to another simple truth - YOU CAN GET EVERYTHING YOU WANT IN LIFE IF YOU HELP ENOUGH OTHER PEOPLE GET WHAT THEY WANT. Grasp that truth, cherish it, - I guarantee the rest of your life will be enlightened.

## *Putting Them To Work*

In some way I was guided towards that philosophy through my early bodybuilding days which created a desire to start my own business and which has given me a very successful chain of health clubs in Great Britain.

I used to train in a little back street gym with sparse equipment and no shower.

Around the age of 17, not long after I started bodybuilding I developed this desire to one day have my own luxury gym and to offer the best fitness training facilities to other people. I knew that many people needed help in achieving pleasant proportions and maintaining health and fitness.

I remembered the early truths I had learned, 'that you could have what you wanted if you really wanted it enough', and I sure wanted that luxury gym badly. Especially whenever I opened the door to that tiny, over crowded, under equipped, back street gym, saturated with the stale smell of sweat.

Through my fondness for reading I also learned the discipline of STUDY to prepare me for success, along with DESIRE, DISCIPLINE AND PATIENCE.

So from the DESIRE stage at 17 years of age I gave PATIENCE, DISCIPLINE and STUDY a pretty good work out and at the age of 30, some 13 years later, I opened my first luxury figure and fitness club. (Being born on the 13th of August I've never been convinced that

13 was an unlucky number.)

When the Bible tells us that, 'he who shall not work shall not eat', I'm sure that the reference is meant for the able bodied, those amongst us who have no genuine reason why they cannot work. Well, there's another simple truth for you, WORK has to be one of the stepping stones towards your Super Successful Life.

You need to work at being healthy. You need to work in order to be wealthy. You need to work to acquire knowledge. Don't chase that 'something for nothing' illusion - it surely does not exist, just ask any successful person!

I set to work when I started my first gym, and I needed to work plenty, because I started with only 100 pounds, that's approximately 200 dollars. Without a lot of work 100 pounds wasn't going to get me very far and in fact it was just about enough to decorate a small office and set up a desk. The rest of the gym came some four months later after I had sold people on enrolling as members in my 'soon to be opened' luxury gym. Thankfully, enough people had faith in me to actually guarantee their membership fee and provided the income to develop all the gym facilities. I achieved this first step by simply getting to work and obtaining all the sales knowledge I could lay my hands on.

Today several thousands of people go through my figure and fitness clubs. We get excellent results for these people so it's certainly proven true for me that, 'you can get everything you want if you will just help enough other people get what they want'. It's a beautiful philosophy.

Along the way so many people, through their teachings and books, have helped me and I am eternally grateful to every one of those people. Some of them have never met me and will have no idea of how their writings have influenced the lives of so many people in a beneficial way. However, I'm sure that somehow they will be deriving an enormous amount of satisfaction from the feeling that they have shared something really worthwhile. The book you have in your hands this very moment will enlighten someone to achieve wonderful things with their life. Will that someone be you?

## Success Must Be Balanced

A Super Successful Life I stress, must be a balanced life, balanced in all the areas physical, mental, spiritual, financial, family and social. Compromise in any of those areas and you'll end up wobbling along life's road like an unbalanced wheel. The super life is for those who work on all six areas.

I have placed the physical first simply because that is my specialty and because in my experience I find that it is a terribly neglected area, even amongst so called successful people.

I have a simple question for those people in terms of their health care. Will you survive your success?

I have explained why I placed the physical first but to be truly practical I should have placed the mental first because truly successful living begins in your mind.

Your mind controls your body

Your mind controls your mouth

Your mind controls your destiny

Your mind determines your attitude

## Super Health and Fitness

The physical aspect of your life requires that you be fit and healthy to ensure your Super Successful Life.

It seems these days that everyone is searching for the secret of fitness and health. Having made a thorough study of this subject I feel I know the way. I know that after much research and experimentation I have a system to provide that which is so earnestly sought after:

life-long fitness and wealth.

Are you ready for the system? Yes, it's a system, not a secret, as Zonnya Harrington in the book PEARL OF POTENTIALITY states.

It has been estimated that over 17,000 different diets have been printed in recent years in various newspapers, etc. Chances are you will have read many of them. After trying to decide which is the best, after trying to decide if jogging is good for you or exercise class or whatever other system that's been suggested to you, I'm going to end all your searching. I'm going to give you the full deal right here. Once again you'll find the system is not complicated just a formula of simple truths.

You develop your super life of health and fitness in body and mind by following this simple formula. Super health and fitness equals ES + SQNF + FS + CPA x PMA. Yes that's it, right there! Now you've got the formula here's what it means.

You develop your super life of health and fitness by (ES) eating slowly and (SQNF) eating small quantities of fresh food as close to the natural state as possible. Plus (FS) good quality food supplements supplying vitamins and minerals plus (CPA) a continuous life of physical activity. Multiplied and enhanced by (PMA) a positive mental attitude. Repeat the formula often ES + SQNF + FS + CPA x PMA = Super health and fitness.

Although I have stressed that you eat as natural a diet as possible, I also recommend vitamin and mineral food supplements as a form of insurance, as it seems well worth the small cost per day to ensure that you are receiving adequate nutrition. That's it! The full formula for super health. Congratulations, you are now on the way to health and fitness and the super living which health and fitness makes possible.

Why do I place so much emphasis on fitness and health for a super successful life? Simply because a sedentary way of life, with very little activity in the form of exercise plus a diet of junky processed foods, eaten in excessive quantities leads to deterioration of the body's vital systems and a depletion of energy. This life style very often leads to FAT and fat kills by putting an extra burden on the heart. Every pound of excess weight causes your heart to pump blood through an extra mile of blood vessels, pumping it to unwanted, unnecessary and unhealthy tissue. If you need to lose 10 or 20 pounds you'll find that losing it will give you a wonderful storehouse of extra energy. In terms of excess fat on the body we can truly say that you achieve more, by losing!

Saving your life is the first step in living an abundant super life. How do we do that? By taking regular exercise and building up gradually from an easy start and reaching a level of exercise that is continuous for a period of at least 10 to 15 minutes and maintaining the heart/pulse rate at 100 to 120 beats per minute, over the full 10 to 15 minute period. There are various kinds of exercises that will enable you to achieve this. Jogging is excellent, Circuit type weight training is superb, the combination of both is magnificent and is ideal for both men and women.

Let me impress upon you that you start easy and gradually and over at least a 5 to 6 week period you reach that desired level of heart/pulse rate. Maintaining this on a regular basis, ideally not less than every other day, will strengthen your heart, making it a stronger more efficient muscular pump to serve your blood circulatory system better. At the same time the strengthened heart will develop a slower relaxed heart beat that reduces the work load and saves wear and tear. A fitness conditioned heart can, within a few weeks, develop a rate that is 10 beats per minute slower than it was prior to your regular fitness program. That simple fact means your heart will be saved from beating over 14,000 times every single day, multiply that by a life time and that leads to a longer, healthier life.

## *The Vibration of Life*

Here's another simple truth. LIFE IS MOVEMENT AND MOVEMENT IS LIFE. Dottie Walters, who inspired me with her vibrant enthusiasm for life, learning and sharing, made me aware that every atom in every cell of the body, is moving at the speed of light, 186,000 miles per second. What a vibrant thought she cultivated in the mind! How could we ever think of ourselves as being tired with all that vibration and energy pulsing within every cell?

The principles I refer to as simple truths are very basic. When you can see the truth in all these principles you will enjoy a healthier, wealthier and wiser life.

## *Mind Power*

There has always been order in the universe and there always will be. When things don't seem in order, realize that the lack of order is not in the universe but in your own attitudes and emotions. When things don't seem just right that's the time to concentrate on your thoughts and feelings. Make sure that what you are concentrating on seems the right thing for you and others. This gets your mind power in order and things start to respond to your ordered mind power.

The natural order of things in the universe reflect freedom and joy and growth through a positive force. Negative emotions and thoughts block the positive aspects of freedom, joy and growth. Negative thoughts and emotions burn up vital energy and contribute to poor health.

You can constantly tear down or build up your health according to your thinking. A wise man said, 'be careful of what you think about because you will surely get it.' Therefore feed your mind with positive, uplifting thoughts. Feed your body with vital nutrients in the form of fresh, good quality foods. Add to your diet, foods such as yogurt, wheat germ and brewers yeast, they have the same positive uplifting effect upon your body that positive thoughts have upon your mind.

Good health is not just an absence of sickness, as many people believe; it is a very positive condition of feeling great. The menu available for your mind and body is exciting and varied and can be a smorgasbord of sheer delight, if you keep searching, learning and growing.

*Keep Moving. Keep Growing!*

The only proof of life is growth - life is a continuous growth process. Keep striving for growth, physical and mental. Don't fall into the trap of 'wishing' for things - work for things and the fuel you need to keep you going is the WÃNT TO. 'Want to' strongly enough that you'll sit down and write down all your goals. Keep looking at those goals. Keep them in a place where you'll constantly have them in sight. Make sure your goals are positive and uplifting and that the achievement of those goals benefits others as well as yourself. With that kind of goal you'll get excited and that in turn will give you that inner encouragement and strength to overcome all the obstacles along the way. When we talk about goals that is the way to achieve them, concentrate not so much on yourself but on others. A surprising thing will happen, - it's not so much what you'll get from reaching your goals but what you'll become by reaching them.

*Simple Truths and Guide Lines*

You can achieve anything you want to if you believe it possible and if you want to strongly enough.
Belief. Discipline. Patience.
What you sow you reap.
What you give out you get back.

You can get everything in life you want if you help enough other people get what they want.

Read. Study. Work.

Mix with and listen to successful people.

Learn from other people's experiences, books, cassettes, seminars, etc.

Life is movement. Movement is life.

The only proof of life is growth.

Observe the order of the universe, tap into this order and develop your own inner order.

$ES + SQNF + FS + CPA \times PMA = A$ super life of health and fitness for body and mind. You're then in the best condition to help others and by helping other people you'll have SUPER WEALTH.

*"Modern man is a giant bestriding the world he has subdued and already reaching out toward other planets, literally new worlds to conquer. But like Samson of old he is a giant who has gone blind. His vision of the spiritual realities summed up for us in Jesus of Nazareth has gone. And like Samson he may pull down upon himself the marvelous temple of civilization which he himself has built. That will inevitably happen unless we get our vision back and make it work."*

*Cecil B. De Mille*

The Enlightenment Amplifiers

BARBARA JUNE HILL
17661 Bouc Raton
Poway, California 92064
(714) 451-0670    (714) 565-1033

## BARBARA JUNE HILL

As President of BJ Hill Consultants, Barbara June Hill is one of the most skilled motivational speakers and stimulating seminar leaders in the field of human relations and personal growth. She is currently a working partner, Vice President and Treasurer of Electronic Metal Fabrication Inc., a leading sheetmetal firm in San Diego, California and President of BarTon-Aire, an airplane leasing firm.

BJ, as she is referred to by many, "is a living example of positive power in motion." She is described as self assured, risk and goal oriented, highly motivated and not thwarted by other people's opinions. Her story of moving from the field of education to the "formidable land of industry" validates a woman of many talents. Coming from "inside herself" she has an incredible, infectious, insatiable enthusiasm for living.

For many years Barbara June Hill has developed insight that produces effectiveness and growth in every aspect of business, professional and personal living as an educator, labor negotiator and now as an executive. Sharing these insights with audiences across the country, using her sparkling wit, powerful speaking voice and down-to-earth common sense to communicate her message, this dynamic woman makes every person relate to her words "don't tell me no" and feel highly motivated to "accomplish whatever it is you want to do with your life."

Barbara June Hill is an author and private pilot. She holds an earned doctorate in Personnel Administration/ Labor Relations from the University of Southern California and is President of the Golden West Region, International Toastmistress Clubs, Inc.

# THE POWER WITHIN

*By Barbara June Hill, Ed.D.*

*"Dip out your ideas like water from a spring. The spring refills and is clearer and so is your mind. The song is more important to the bird than to the hearer. Does the evening thrush sing for you or even for his mate?....he responds to the purple twilight with silver notes. He sings for himself."*
   Henry Seidel Canby

*Decide For Yourself That You're Important*

I've cleaned your catbox, now may I go? There I was on my knees sifting the cat litter, tears streaming down my face when finally in anger, frustration and disbelief, I shouted "WHY AM I DOING THIS? THESE AREN'T EVEN MY CATS!" Perhaps the "catbox story" represents the way you feel about the situation you find yourself in today.

Have you ever felt second rate, filling everyone else's needs first and maybe, if there's time, you are allowed to do something that you want to do? Have you folded shorts "in thirds", being sure the label is in the back, that they are right side out, placed neatly in the drawer and not touching the undershirts? (Yours waiting until tomorrow because time ran out). Then you have experienced the catbox. Sorry to say "WE HAVE MET THE ENEMY AND IT IS US" as Pogo would say.

Stand up for yourself. Begin in small things like sending the steak back that was not cooked "as ordered". When you are asked to go someplace and you truly do not wish to do so, say "NO," even if you are the only one in the group. You've been programmed to "go along with the group", "be a sport" or "fit in and make everyone happy". Remember that you pass this way but once and that time is yours and you are important, SAY THAT YOU'RE IMPORTANT.    WILL THE REAL YOU PLEASE STAND UP?


*You Are Where You Are, Doing What You Want to Do, or You'd Change It!*

If you're unhappy with your job, in a relationship that doesn't suit you, or out of money, you have erroneously placed emphasis on lack, self worthlessness and disharmony. You're in your environment by your own choice and if you truly don't like it, you will do one of two things: you will continue to wallow in it or you will change your course by altering your thought toward yourself, other people and things. Extremely important is knowing and understanding that whatever is happening to you today is of your own creation. You are reaping what you have sowed. Negative thought patterns bring limitation and defeatism and positive thought patterns provide inspiration and prosperity.

*Laying the Groundwork*

What do you mean you don't like your job? You selected it! "I'd still be happily married if it hadn't been for my husband, or wife, or mother. If the kids hadn't come along I would have been a lot farther down the road than I am today! OR If I had more money, look at the things that I could do!" The truth is you chose to be a wife or husband or to have kids. You've chosen the job you hold and you choose to stay, believe it or not! If you are out of money, you have selected that too and slammed the door on yourself. You have placed yourself today where you are at this moment by your own past decisions. What's more frightening, you have already chosen what your tommorow will be like by your thoughts today. Have you chosen lack, or prosperity? love or hatred? dead ends or alternatives? depression or spontaneity? YOU ARE AN EXTREMELY POWERFUL PERSON.

*Exercising Your Options*

It has been said of me that I am a successful person. Yes, by most everyone's standards I am successful because I like myself, know where I am going and as one of my close friends said about me, "You seem to MELT THE MOUNTAINS". So it has been ever thus, turning what seemed to be adversity into success from the beginning. Born of the depression, food in brown paper bags and my mother and sister and me alone as a team, one might suspect that each of us would have emerged negative, selfish and withdrawn.

While material things were short we were "long" on love and inner strength. We knew we were never really alone and when the "going got tough" that by continuing to trust and send positive thoughts and requests, as promised, they would be returned ten fold to fill our needs. I can remember more than once returning from church and finding a loaf of bread and a dozen eggs hugging our front doorstep. We were expectant and grateful. Help was, and is, all around. Lack and limitation exist only in the mind. Exercise your option to be a winner for yourself, I DARE YOU!

*Know That You Can Do Anything You Truly Want To Do*

Learn to tell the difference between wishing and wanting. Wishing is something that you do with the Sears Roebuck catalog. My sister and I used to play "dibs" with the catalog since dollars were short and laughter and loving long. She would pick choices from the left side of the page and I the right and "Wish" that we could have something on the page. That's wishing. It's like "Wishing you could have a million dollars". Now conversely, if you told me that you WANTED a million dollars, THAT'S DIFFERENT! You would be saying that you are willing to put time, effort and even money into the process of gaining it and IT BECOMES POSSIBLE. Remember, TIME, EFFORT AND MONEY, if necessary. Go back to the basic questions again. Do you wish or want a new or different job? Do you wish or want to go back to school? Do you wish or want a positive relationship? Do you wish or want more money? Begin testing all of your thinking, am I WISHING OR WANTING? If you truly WANT to accomplish something, it is done! It has already occurred. All you must do is accept it and collect.

*Take Action on a Goal or Goals in Your Life*

Do you have something in your life that's important to you to accomplish? I was in a very long, heavy labor relations negotiating session as a negotiator and things looked particularly dark and immovable. Suddenly I knew that for me to be useful to the process I needed to allow some new ideas to flow into my consciousness to energize "my reserve tank". I needed to come to "the table" with some possible alternative solutions for the benefit of everyone.

Pushing myself back from the desk, I called Gillespie Air Field, (a general aviation field in San Diego) and said "Rev something up out there, I'll be there in 10 minutes and I want to be in the air with an instructor. IT'S TIME FOR ME TO ACCOMPLISH THE GOAL TO LEARN TO FLY!

The next 30 days "lunch" was in the air learning the intricacies of flying a single engine Piper 140 airplane. Today I fly my own plane wherever and whenever I want to BECAUSE I PUT POSITIVE POWER THINKING BEHIND A GOAL. I aspired to something that I wanted to do. If you have no plan or direction in your life, you will arrive exactly there, NO PLACE. Then you are decaying, dying and taking up space. ARE YOU AMONG THE LIVING? WELL, ARE YOU?

*Accept Only Positive Alternatives*

Oft times people give up too soon. When someone says "it can't be done", my whole being responds in a "SEZ WHO?" As a Senior music student in college, my instructor was irate with me and said, "If you think you're so good, why don't you audition for Roger Wagner (conductor of the Roger Wagner Chorale)? You won't make it." You guessed it, not only did I audition but sang for five years with the Chorale doing symphony concerts in the Hollywood Bowl and with the Los Angeles Symphony, cutting records for CBS and recording background music for pictures at Fox Studios. YOU NEVER KNOW WHAT YOU CAN DO until the challenge is levied and you decide to "make space for yourself."

There is never a lack of ideas nor are there any dead ends unless you agree to it. One door closes and another one is standing ajar waiting for your grasp. That's like saying to me that I couldn't get the airplane from San Diego to the Grand Canyon by myself that first flying year. Not only was the trip an exciting learning experience (I'd never landed on an icy runway before) but the New Year's Eve party there was fun.
ACCEPT ONLY POSITIVE POSSIBLE
ALTERNATIVES.

*Carry Only Your Share of the Load*

Either you are in control of how you will spend your time or others will control you. Bill Oncken, a leading management consultant says in his Time Management training, "Don't take other people's monkeys". It is so true. I was Assistant Superintendent of Personnel for the Grossmont Unified School District and often I worked with Dr. John Barrons, Assistant Superintendent of Business. John was a past master at "giving away monkeys". He'd call me on the telephone and say "We have a problem". Depending on how I answered that question, the monkey could put two feet on my shoulder. Assuming that I agreed that the problem was "ours" jointly, the other two feet would clamp ferociously on my shoulder if I "agreed to research the problem and get back" to John. Meanwhile, he would play golf. How often and how quickly we agree "to help" and then wonder at the end of the day why we didn't get it all accomplished. Be selective and set your priorities. Just as important as knowing what's important in life is knowing what isn't important. AND WATCH OUT FOR THE MONKEYS.

*Get To the Bottom of the Boat*

When the wars and turmoils of daily life seem to be

uncontrollable FIND TIME FOR YOURSELF BY YOURSELF--Get to the bottom of the boat - seek quiet and listen. Most of us holler and scream when the place gets wild and it's just exactly the opposite of where we should be. If it's transcendental meditation or yoga or "just plain finding a quiet place" out of doors, (perhaps listening to some quiet music), do whatever it is that allows you time to regroup and slowly assess where you are and where you want to go from here.

Start with one corner of your environment; a desk maybe, or that letter that you've been going to write or just paying the bills. Just start ONE thing and get it finished and mailed or delivered. A friend of mine once described it at its best. "Look to the Chinese - When faced with a whole rice field to plant, they never look up at the field and establish the "I'll never make it" syndrome. They plant one plant carefully, then the second and another until the first row is complete. Turning patiently, now the first plant in the second row, and finally, the last plant in the field. The field is finished! One step at a time and you are again in the driver's seat. OUT OF THE CONFUSION AND INTO CONTROL ONCE MORE. There is ebb and flow in our lives and the patience and understanding of that simple fact will save much anguish. Sometimes it means just sitting still and allowing the simple morning sounds of the birds chattering as the dawn breaks to flood a weary spirit. They are so expectant, full of love and excitement for the day. Tho' it be their last, it will be a glorious day begun in the light of dawn. All too soon the drumming of a car engine will blot out this serenity with someone who has "hurried" into the day. James Allen in "AS A MAN THINKETH" shares "Calmness is power. Say unto your heart, 'Peace be still!'"

## All the Abundance You Need

For some reason what seems to be a lack of money is

one of the biggest hurdles for us to jump. Money is but energy. Energy is but positive idea. If there is not enough money, there is a lack of positive energy - positive thought for the base of the generation of positive action. If your life is devoted to negative thinking, I can't, it won't, "they've stopped me", then your energy or source is negative and your plight is lack. Conversely, if your thought or energy base is positive, the "action base" is positive, the energy will be positive and a plethora of ideas will bring more money and material wealth than you can envision.

YOU ARE WHERE YOU ARE, DOING WHAT YOU WANT TO DO, OR YOU'D CHANGE IT! Reflect the quality of your life. The power of your thought gives form to your ideas and provides the environment in which you live. Surround yourself with an abundant life, a constant flow of ideas and an unceasing source of positive energy. Then you are centering on a constructive purpose. Believe it; know and expect that it will occur.

Determine your life success by design, not by chance. The commitment to the excellence of living requires that you prepare for change, rise above the wayward winds and accomplish what you set out to do. TAKE CHARGE OF TOMORROW, NOW!

POSITIVE POWER PEOPLE
The Enlightenment Amplifiers

**JOY GROSS, DIRECTOR**
Pawling Health Manor
Box 401
Hyde Park, N.Y. 12538

## JOY GROSS

Joy Gross is the owner-director of the world famous health retreat, the Pawling Health Manor in Hyde Park, New York. Joy co-founded the retreat (often known as the "Last Resort") with Dr. Robert Gross, the Manor's nutritional consultant, in 1959. Since then more than 35,000 guests have come to the Manor for rejuvenation and weight reduction. In addition to managing the Manor, Joy conducts several workshops each week for the Manor's guests, including an elegant weekly food demonstration-buffet. She conducts a monthly reinforcement group in New York City and is the author of the successful health and diet book, "The 30-Day Way to a Born-Again Body" (Rawson-Wade, N.Y., to be published this spring in paperback by Berkley.) She has lectured and done radio, television and newspaper interviews extensively throughout the United States and in Canada. She is a member of National Speakers Association.

Joy was born 52 years ago in Winchester, Kentucky. She is proud of her five glowingly healthy children who range in age from 17 to 32.

## 11

### POSITIVE POWER PEOPLE
*The Enlightenment Amplifiers*

# POWER IS LIFE

*By Joy Gross*

*"Dream lofty dreams, and as you dream, so shall you become. Your vision is the promise of what you shall one day be. Your ideal is the prophecy of what you shall at last unveil."*
   *James Allen*

POWER is awesome. POWER is energy. POWER is life!

It has taken me half a century to learn how to use the power of the life-force of the Universe consciously to effect changes in my life. While I have made use of that power throughout my life, I've done so in a totally haphazard, undirected, unconscious way. When an obstacle would come along, I'd tap into my power line. In between crises, I'd coast along in low gear, totally unaware of my power-pattern.

For almost 30 years my major involvement was my

family and home. I expended most of my conscious
energy on being the best housewife and mother I knew
how to be. By the age of 49, except for a brief period when
I was a teenager, I had never earned money on my own.
The thought of financial self-responsibility petrified me
and led me to accept a dependent role, financially and in
other ways, in my marriages. While part of me accepted
this role, another self was deeply resentful. After my
second marriage, my husband Robert and I established a
health retreat along the banks of the Hudson River in
upstate New York. I devoted myself totally, working long
hours, weeks, months and years, while caring for my, and
later, our children, in addition. However, I had no power
in the management of our retreat. I saw many ways it
could have been managed with greater efficiency and
beauty. I gradually withdrew from the business in order
to avoid conflict. I assuaged my self-esteem by doing
volunteer work in various organizations. My proudest
moments were basking in the reputation Robert was
gaining through his total dedication to the health and
weight problems of Manor guests.

A few years ago I began to slip into a mild depression
from time to time. I'd wake up in the early hours of
morning and starkly ponder the fact that my most
productive years were sliding away from me and that I
wasn't really using my creative abilities except in a
nurturing way in behalf of my family. "Is this all there
is?" I'd ask myself. I began to read during the nights
when I'd wake up with what I called my "ball of fire" in
my chest. One day I took an old book from the bookcase
in our den. It was "Power of Will" by Robert Collier. I
ended up not just reading, but re-reading and marking
phrases which seemed to have been written just for me:

*"We float along carrying out other people's will simply
because our own will has become scotched and dormant
from lack of use...If you can't lift up your head and tell
the world you're good - if you can't drive home your ideas*

*with a thud that makes your presence felt where you want it felt - if you can't set your eyes on a certain goal and ride roughshod over all obstacles until you hit the tape - in short, if you haven't got a firm, unbreakable will-power to help you smash discouragement and trample down opposition - then you're going to drop down and you're going to keep down... You must exercise your constructive ability in designing, planning, mapping out and making a working diagram of that which you wish to accomplish."*

And, in the following chapter, some thoughts on paying the price.

*"In all attainment, the 'price' must be paid."*

The thought of paying a price for gaining more control over my life frightened me. I cringed at the thought of what my price would be. I knew I wanted to be financially independent; somehow I knew that unless you can take care of yourself, you can never be truly independent or free to be who you really are. I couldn't see quite how I could ever do it. I feared losing my home; I had visions of being dependent forever. But then, haven't we women been conditioned to think that way from early childhood? Haven't we been told that "The father is the head of the house" and "The husband is the provider" and "The woman's place is in the home?"

My head would pound, my chest would fairly explode, as I read and pondered. I read book after book. Gradually inspiration began to replace depression. Goals began to take shape in my mind.

I'd nagged Bob to write a book for years. He had great knowledge and experience in the field of nutrition and weight control. I was sure he could write a book that would be a winner. He had no interest in the project.

One day, like a bolt out of the blue, I asked myself, "Why don't YOU write a book?"

I'd been giving a weekly class in nutrition at the Manor for three years. I'd studied biochemistry, and had lived the principles of Natural Hygiene since I was a teenager.

Our guests were eager for information to incorporate into their lives when they returned home.

I met with a friend, Collette Dowling, who's a successful writer. I asked her to help me with my project. Together we worked on an outline, got an agent, and within an amazingly short period of time, I'd sold my idea and myself to a major New York publisher (Rawson-Wade). My agent negotiated for a generous advance. On the day the acceptance letter came from the publisher, I felt I was living a dream. I was elated. It was a turning-point in my life.

Looking back, I can see that subconsciously I've developed a pattern in the overcoming of obstacles in my life. Though I was unaware on a conscious level of what was happening, I was "tapping in" to my power-line on an emergency basis. For example (and this is going back to my earliest memories), when I was a toddler my black iron crib sat in a corner of my parents' bedroom, next to a window where I could peek out and watch other kids playing outside. When mother put me in for my afternoon nap, I'd much rather have been outside with the other children. I discovered that if I stood up and shook the side panel of the crib long and hard enough, the safety catch would give and the side would go down. I could then escape! I was tapping my power-source.

One of the most serious obstacles I faced was an "incurable" skin disease, psoriasis. When I was nine, the skin specialist my mom took me to made a grim pronouncement.

"There's no known cause and no known cure," he said. "Joy will just have to learn to live with it."

Later on my mom became friends with a neighbor, a young widow, mother of four, whose overweight husband had died of a heart attack. Her family doctor suggested that Margaret had contributed to her husband's problem by feeding him a diet too rich in all the foods most women delight in serving their families: rich desserts, steaks, hot breads, gravies, spicy foods and such. (After all, isn't that one of the best ways to show love)?

Margaret began seeking a more healthful way to feed her family. She began to stress salads, fruits and vegetables. She shared her ideas with mother. Mother encouraged me to be careful about my diet - maybe it would help my skin. I didn't want to be different from my friends, and besides, I was addicted to my favorite junk foods.

The summer I was 14 I visited with relatives for the summer. They plied me with all the goodies I could ever want. I was in my glory! That summer my skin became miserably worse. When I returned home at the end of the summer, the ugly red lesions were so severe that people would turn and stare at me as I walked on the street. I became thoughtful, finally, of the information mother had attempted to have me share with her. I began to read and learn more about a new, more healthful way of life. I poured through books by unorthodox but powerful leaders in the field of Natural Hygiene, a health science which includes fasting, right thinking, exercise, fresh air, and sunshine as its basic premise. I committed myself to give it a try, even though the specialists had said that there was no cure for my condition. I was determined to do anything hopeful to try to change my skin from ugly to normal. I wanted desperately to be what I knew I was designed to be - attractive and acceptable. Once again, I tapped into my power-supply.

In time, my new living habits allowed me to keep my skin clear. I regained my self-confidence and devoted a major part of my life to the study of health and nutrition. I fell by the wayside from time to time, but would always get back up and start over again. The longer I stayed with it, the easier it became to adhere to the regime. I proved that sticking to a diet of predominantly fresh fruits and vegetables and incorporating all the other health disciplines into my everyday life enabled me to have healthy, smooth skin and vibrant health.

I got married to a handsome vegetarian when I was nineteen. We had three children. My first, a son, suffered a lack of oxygen during birth; as a result, he was slow to learn. When he was five years old I was told by the principal of the special school he was enrolled in that he was uneducable. Later, after his father and I were divorced and I'd moved to upstate New York, I was fortunate to seek - and find - a very special private school run by some very special people who had faith, as I did, that Louie was indeed educable. I tapped in again! I learned that he had impaired vision as a result of broken blood vessels behind his eyes - damage that had occurred at birth. He was fitted with corrective lenses, after which his school work improved. That little boy who was supposedly uneducable now reads voraciously, has a twelve-year employment record in our local hospital, is self-supporting, and maintains a lovely apartment.

Through my involvement with a local organization devoted to educating and training exceptional children and adults, I was elected to its Board of Directors and served two consecutive three-year terms. I also served a total of ten years on the Board of Directors of the American Natural Hygiene Society, a national health organization headquartered in Bridgeport, Conn.. I served as their national convention program chairperson for four years.

My involvement in these community and national organizations helped me to develop poise and self-confidence I would never have thought possible in my early life. I've given talks at conventions and other gatherings through the years, but until I began to lecture on a regular weekly basis at the Health Manor, I never felt at ease on the platform. Every week I'd face our overweight guests with a bit of fear and trembling, often forgetting my train of thought. I kept working at it and kept improving.

Just before my book came out, my publishers asked me to accompany them to a sales conference at the Harvard Club in New York City where I was to give a talk to 50 book salesmen from Scribner's whose job it was, as distributors, to get bookstores throughout the country to stock my book. My mouth was dry, my heart was thumping fiercely within my chest, but I overcame the urge to panic. I must exert POWER over these men, I told myself. I stood in front of them, finally calm, enthusiastic, looking thin, healthy, and I was told, younger by far than my fifty years. I tapped in to my power-line. My enthusiasm and control of my subject and subjects paid off. Two months later as I visited major bookstores during my 15-city major publicity tour, I was thrilled to see stacks of books with my picture on the front cover staring back at me from bookshelves. It was almost as if I were in a dream. I remembered myself forty years earlier, dreaming of someday becoming famous, of writing a book, of doing great things to help people, of one day owning a beautiful home, driving a good car, but most important, being able to influence people. "I did it," I smiled to myself as I autographed books for customers.

My cross-country tour taught me a great deal about poise and power. I've done over 150 television, radio, and newspaper interviews, over 100 on my three week tour. There were so many cities to cover, so many shows staggered one next to the other, that I actually didn't have time to be nervous. I simply plunged in and met the challenge! I tapped in once more. Had I not had a thorough knowledge of my subject, a deep conviction of the truth of that knowledge, and been living proof of it's efficacy, I could not have handled it. I had outstanding write-ups in major newspapers such as the Los Angeles Herald-Examiner, the Oakland Tribune, the Ft. Worth Star Telegram, the St. Paul Pioneer Press, the Philadelphia Daily News, the Gannett chain, the Buffalo Courier-Journal, the Arkansas Gazette, the Houston Post and others. Excerpts from my book were printed in Self magazine, New Woman, Beauty Digest, Library Journal, Family Health, Star, Grit, and others.

My power had become magnified.

It's a powerfully good feeling to know you are influencing thousands of people not only nationally but internationally as well. The hardcover of The 30-Day Way to a Born-Again body, went through six printings; paperback will be published in the spring and given much wider distribution. I shall always remember the day last March when a pile of my books was featured in a window display at Scribner's on Fifth Avenue in New York.

Flashbacks slid across the screen of my mind. I saw the times my then considered austere eating and living habits and my dedication to the pursuit of healthful living set me apart from my peers; when I had allowed myself to feel different and isolated; when I was apologetic about my way of life. Now, looking in the window at Scribner's, I felt power and pride that I'd come full circle and was looked up to as an authority in my field.

In the last two years I have become owner as well as director of the Pawling Health Manor. A year ago, I assumed full responsibility for the total operation of the year-round retreat where over 35,000 people over the last 20 years have become slim and rejuvenated. The financial responsibility for the operation was the step that required the most courage as I assumed total responsibility for myself for the first time in my life. I've learned throughout the year that the self-confidence and expertise I'd learned simply by meeting the challenges of growth as they came along, flowed over into the world of finance as well. It was a Powerfully nice feeling!

Health is wholeness. Being healthy requires an awareness first of all of what health - life - is all about. It gives you power over your physical body. One of the first laws of health I learned 40 years ago when my search for self-power began, was that life is based on awesome immutable laws. Ignorance of those laws does not excuse anyone from the consequences of the non-application of or the breaking of those laws. Recognition of the Law of Life, a search to find Truth, application of truth to your life, applies on all levels, physical, mental and spiritual. Cooperation with the immutable laws of the Universe will help keep you well, young and beautiful, physically, emotionally and spiritually.

The obstacles I've had to overcome in my life have led me to search for answers, for ways to overcome those obstacles. Through the years I've become more and more aware of the vastness of the supply of power within universal intelligence from which to draw. I have learned that to reach your goals you have to continue to draw upon those universal sources. That this process requires effort, it requires dedication, it requires vision.

I have learned that you have to be aware of your own potential for success and for greatness. I have learned that as you acquire knowledge, you have more to share with others; that as they begin to grow and to share, your influence becomes a radiance that helps to brighten the darkness of illness and ignorance in this world.

If you would like to find new happiness, health and freedom, I urge you to begin to make changes starting now. Set new goals for yourself. Tune in to the power-lines that are available to you. Make a commitment to yourself; begin your journey now. If I did it, you can do it, too!

*"If I were going to college today and could take with me any one piece of equipment, I would ask for an adventurous mind."*
                    *Cecile B. DeMille*

The Enlightenment Amplifiers

JEROME MURRAY, Ph.D.
Jerome Murray Consulting Resources
19545 Miller Ct.
Saratoga, California 95070
(408) 446-5160

## DR. JEROME MURRAY

It's a long way from J.D. (juvenile delinquent) to Ph.D. It's a trip that appeals, however, when you've almost been killed in a gang fight, dropped out of high school, turned down an offer to go to Annapolis, flunked the highest school in the military for enlisted men and ended up scrubbing the latrine.

The decision to make that trip moved Jerome Murray from a 19 year old, taking stock of himself on a Navy bunk to the Honorman of another Naval training school and valedictorian of his doctoral class. Dr. Murray is now a nationally recognized clinical psychologist, management consultant, professional speaker and author. Halfway down the road, he sang professionally on stage, had his own radio and TV shows and recorded an album.

Founder and Executive Director of Guidance Associates, Dr. Murray has for many years had a successful private practice in psychotherapy. As his reputation and the demand for his services grew he founded Jerome Murray Consulting Resources, a management consulting firm. His training publications, the CARE book, the Laymen's Guide to Mental Disorders, the Counseling Interview, the Selection Interview, and the CALM technique, have had wide application and acceptance in his many management seminars. He is listed in "Who's Who in Finance and Industry".

With a doctoral dissertation on the development of self-esteem and many years as a successful psychotherapist, Dr. Murray's reputation as a personal development expert is well deserved. His Guidance Tape

Library has numerous titles in self-improvement from "Living with Myself and Liking It", to "The Devil Made Me Do It".

It seems only natural that with a background in the entertainment industry the road would lead to public speaking. One of the most sought after members of the National Speakers Association, his enthusiastic, humorous style of imparting concrete, useable information gets him invited back again and again.

Not just a consultant or psychologist, he is an advocate of the marriage between psychology and philosophy bringing insight to the laws that govern business and personal success.

*"To be what we are, and to become what we are capable of becoming, is the only end of life."*
                    *Benedict de Spinoza*

# THE POWER OF DOING IT NOW

*by Jerome Murray, Ph.D.*

*"If a man look sharply and attentively, he shall see fortune; for though she is blind, she is not invisible."*
*Francis Bacon*

If you've gotten this far, be encouraged. A serious procrastinator would never get around to reading this book. One person told me, "don't mess with my procrastination, it's the only rest I get." Aside from the humorous acceptance that most of us have regarding procrastination, the actual facts aren't funny. Procrastination is the biggest thief in the history of mankind. It has robbed people of success, happiness and fulfillment, in their personal, family and business lives. The best motivation lecture in the world cannot hold a candle to the power of procrastination. Because it's such a powerful force in our life, I don't expect that you'll become a person who never procrastinates. In fact, I encourage you to procrastinate in a constructive way - put off procrastination! Procrastination is more than simply putting things off, however. It involves a multitude of strategies for avoiding the completion of any task. Everything from dawdling, delaying, negativism, pseudoperfectionism, forgetting, running away and various side-tracking strategies all are examples of procrastination. Procrastination is any conscious or unconscious attempt to avoid the completion of a task that we ostensibly desire to perform.

## How to Put Off Procrastination

The first step in dealing with procrastination is to understand the basic underlying reason for it. It is not laziness, sloth or irresponsibility that produces procrastination. Basically, procrastination is an attempt by the individual to protect self-esteem. It may be a misguided attempt, but the intention is honorable. When we procrastinate regarding a task, it is because the completion of the task has an implicit threat to our self-esteem.

There are three basic causes for procrastination and all of them are efforts to protect the life blood of the personality - self-esteem.

## PASSIVE - AGGRESSION

Passive-aggression is a method of expressing anger toward an authority figure on whom we are overly- , dependent. Many times in a relationship such as with a parent or employer, anger is stimulated that we fear expressing because we can't afford to lose the relationship. Therefore, all of us at one time or another, have learned to express anger passively - that is to express it toward the authority figure in a disguised form so that neither we nor the authority figure recognize it as anger. Two things can create passive-aggression.

*Pressure and Procrastination*

Many people grow up in a constant atmosphere of pressure and overcoercion. From awakening in the morning until going to bed at night, they are subjected to a constant barrage of commands. "It's time to get up, now brush your teeth." "Don't wear those, they're dirty." "Hurry up and eat your breakfast." "Don't use your spoon, use your fork." "Don't bend over, you'll get hunchback." "Now get to school, you'll be late." "Don't forget your books." "Wipe your feet when you come in." "Remember your homework." "How many times have I told you take out the garbage." "Hurry up you'll be late to dinner." "Don't come with your hands dirty, wash your hands." "Eat all of your vegetables." "Quit watching TV, it's time to go to bed." "Be sure to clean up before you go to bed." "Now get to sleep, don't just lie there." This form of parental anxiety about a child's welfare is an environment that many people lived with 24 hours out of every day. Even in their dreams, they were being ordered around. Pressure like this creates a threat to a child's autonomy which is a significant part of self-esteem. To protect one's autonomy, the right to make choices, the child learns to aggress against the parent in passive ways. Dawdling, delaying, and forgetting are all expressions by the child of the subconscious desire to say, "I don't want to, get off my back!"

When this child becomes an adult, two things characteristically occur. Any relationship with an authority figure creates the anticipation of being pressured and may stimulate a rebellion even when no actual demands have been made. The second thing that occurs is that they internalize the pressure and demands they grew up with and perpetuate the problem by continuing to pressure and coerce themselves.

A businessman who consulted with me discovered this as the cause of his procrastination. When I asked him to record his internal dialogue for a full day's time, he discovered that from morning until night he was subjecting himself to a constant harangue of pressure, demands, expectations, "shoulds," "oughts," and "musts." I then asked him, "what do you think would happen if you talked to an employee the way you talked to yourself?" His spontaneous answer was "why he would quit." A burst of enlightenment hit him and he said, "that's what I've done, haven't I? I've quit!"

If you find that you are constantly putting pressure on yourself to succeed, to work harder, to get more done, or to not be lazy; you will create a command-resistance cycle. One part of your mind will be demanding and haranguing, and the other part of your mind, through procrastination, will be saying, "drop dead!" Procrastination is an attempt by the individual to protect self-esteem in the form of autonomy. You not only have a right, you have a *need* to know that you can make choices.

*Punishment and Procrastination*

Many children grow up constantly afraid of being punished for wrongdoing. This punishment may come in the form of physical punishment, such as beating, spanking, slapping, or kicking, or it may be verbal punishment in the form of constant criticism. "It's all your fault." "Why didn't you do it right?" "What a stupid thing to do." "Don't be a baby." "Would you look at that." "Well have you ever." "You are a bad child." Many parents believe that you can make a child better by physically or verbally "beating the devil out of them." Others simply use the children as scapegoats.

If you suffered from this unfair and unjust form of punishment, you may experience a burning desire to get even. But how does a child get even with their parents? One method is sure fire. You can always depend upon the fact that your parents wanted you to function; get good grades, perform chores and be a good child. The method for getting even, therefore, is to not function. Don't get good grades, don't perform the chores, or do anything that will give them pleasure. You may have continued this pattern now that you're an adult. On the one hand, you blame, name-call, ridicule, and shame yourself for not functioning or performing adequately, and on the other hand, you continue to get even against that punishment by not functioning. The pattern is what I call the "darned if I will, and admit I wasn't " syndrome.

Let's assume, for instance, that you have the best of intentions of doing something very kind for someone. You're feeling grateful, appreciative and caring. About the time that you're deciding exactly what it is that you will do, imagine that someone coming up to you, verbally berating, accusing and punishing you for being unkind and insensitive. Now what do you feel like doing? You probably don't feel too loving. For you to do something at that point, as you originally had intended, you would have to admit by implication that their accusations were correct. You were unkind and insensitive and you wouldn't have done it if they hadn't pointed that out. "Darned if I will, and admit that I wasn't" is the thought that produces procrastination.

When the doing of something makes the punishing authority right, you'll procrastinate. When the doing of something makes a punishing authority feel pleasure, you'll procrastinate. When the doing of something demands that you admit that you're bad, you'll procrastinate. This form of procrastination is an attempt to get revenge on the punishing authority by not functioning as the authority wishes you to. The problem, of course, is that the punishing authority is no longer around and the only one getting hurt is you. It is an attempt to protect self-esteem by refusing to engage in behaviors that would be the implicit acceptance of a negative status. "Darned if I will, and admit I wasn't."

## FEAR OF SUCCESS

Ironically, while almost everyone talks about wanting to be a success, some people actually fear it. The attainment of success represents a threat to them that they unconsciously avoid by procrastination.

### Feeling Unworthy

Some homes are dominated by an atmosphere of sin and punishment. When you're bad, you must be punished. As adults, these individuals feel guilty most of the time. Because of real or imagined wrongdoing, they feel deserving of punishment. Therefore, they punish themselves by not permitting themselves to be successful. When they are successful, they feel an increased sense of unworthiness. When given congratulations or compliments, they respond with, "Thanks, but I really don't deserve it."

Others have a deep-seated and usually unquestioned belief that to be successful is to be sinful. They've been taught that the successful people of this world got that way because of sin and corruption and that righteous people are all poor and suffering. As adults, these individuals may talk of success and make efforts to attain it, but in actual fact, they consistently defeat themselves so that they can be poor, suffering, and righteous. The cliche, "God must have loved poor people because he made so many of them," is an implicit   acknowledgement of the idea that righteousness and poverty go together.

### Breaking the Family Pattern

This is another example of how guilt produces procrastination. This is an unconscious use of procrastination to avoid success because significant others are not successful. John B. consulted with me because of his erratic behavior in college. In the early years he worked hard and got good grades, but the closer he got to graduation, the more he found himself avoiding homework and attending class. Completely confused and bewildered, because consciously he wanted to graduate, he sought therapy. John's father, whom he dearly loved, had never graduated from college. Unconsciously, John saw graduation from college as too great an achievement and viewed it as a repudiation of his father who didn't even finish high school.

Here is a diagnostic clue for you. Imagine that you are more successful and "better" than your parents. If you find yourself vaguely uncomfortable with that idea, and sense that you want to resist it, you could be a victim of the fear of success. Be careful that you don't attempt to validate a parent's life by duplicating it. Remember that the success of the child is not a negation, but an affirmation of the parent.

## Playing Second Fiddle

Procrastination can be the result of a child's forced subordination to a power-hungry parent. Consider the parent whose self-concept is one of confidence and adequacy; so much that they walk into areas of responsibility where most angels fear to tread. They have such an intense need for recognition that they are compulsively driven to do well. Since they avoid anxiety by maintaining superiority, they place their children in a horrendous double-bind. Because they fear and despise weakness, they demand that their child excel. But as soon as the child begins to succeed, the power-hungry parent feels their superiority threatened, turns on the child, and criticizes their efforts. This puts the child in an impossible position. They're criticized if they don't learn and develop - and criticized if they do. As adults, these people feel anxiety whenever they begin to approach success. Success is associated with the wrath and criticism of a now absent parent, and fear is generated whenever it is imminent. Because of this fear of success, procrastination becomes the method of choice in avoiding it.

*Comfortable Mediocrity*

As strange as it may seem, some people are afraid of success because it would be too much effort to change from mediocrity to success. Being successful means more than just having more money and living in a finer home. There are all kinds of behavior that are attendant to any lifestyle. When a person becomes successful, there are many things that change in their life. New friends, new attitudes, new lifestyle and new responsibilities. It can be quite comfortable to be mediocre and many people, while fantasizing about success, in reality don't want to expend the effort to obtain it. In our culture, not wishing to be successful is tantamount to cursing the flag, motherhood and apple pie. These individuals satisfy the conflict by talking about success, wishing out loud that they had it, bemoaning their fate because they don't, and procrastinating to avoid it.

## FEAR OF FAILURE

In the truest sense, we don't fear failure, we fear the consequences of failure. When failure is associated with criticism or rejection, we fear failure because we don't want those consequences. We would have little trouble with failure if we simply viewed it as a process of elimination on the road to success.

*Protecting Self-worth*

Many children are raised under circumstances of

conditional regard. Conditional regard is when the parents regard the child as worthy only when the child meets certain conditions. The conditions may be anything from getting good grades to making the team, to working around the house. But the attitude is always the same. The child only has worth when the conditions are met. If you attach your worth to achievement, you can be paralyzed by procrastination. How much achievement is enough? At what level of achievement will you feel worthy? Here the person is in a real quandary. On the one hand they feel unworthy if they don't achieve certain things - on the other hand, they fear the possibility of failure which might prove that they will never be worthy.

To deal with this dilemma, procrastinators have become adept at certain strategies. One of these is *The Perpetual Preparation Strategy*. In this strategy, the individual avoids the final fear of evaluation by always being in preparation to achieve, but never finishing anything completely. One man that I saw used this strategy in the form of becoming an eternal student. In reality, he had a rather mundane job, which gave him no sense of status or attainment. His worth was protected by the fact that he was going to school to get a degree, at which time he would do something truly worthwhile and valuable. Upon attainment of his first degree, fearful of going out and putting his worth on the line, he decided that he needed another degree. So again, he was in preparation to achieve and could not be evaluated for what he had actually done. By the time I finally saw him, he was 50 years of age, had four degrees and hadn't done anything yet. By this time his strategy was becoming plain, even to himself, and he was considerably depressed. In actual fact, he was a charming, likable man, who had considerably more success than the average person. But because his needs were so great, he unconsciously sensed that he would never measure up to his ideal. The only solution left to him was to avoid the trauma of failure by perpetual preparation.

The fear of failure fosters another popularly used strategy called *The Dependency Strategy.* Here the individual procrastinates with the unspoken belief that if he waits long enough, someone else will do it for him. As adults, they usually find themselves married to "rescuers" who end up carrying the brunt of the responsibility in the relationship. The procrastinator puts things off long enough so that the tension becomes unbearable to the "rescuer" who rushes in and completes the task.

## The Perils of Perfectionism

Perfectionism is very similar to protecting self-worth but with an ironic twist. Unlike the individual who sets high standards of excellence, attains them, and feels satisfied; the perfectionist sets high standards, attains them, and is dissatisfied. He concludes that the standards were probably too low. New, higher standards are set, but always just out of reach, leaving the perfectionist perpetually disappointed and frustrated.

The perfectionist, as a child, usually had "billy goat" parents. Every offer of praise was paired with a "but." "That's a good job - *but...*" "It's fine - *but...*" These parents "butted" their children to death. Upon bringing home a report card, the parent wants to know why the "D" wasn't a "C". The child receives a "C" and "the C is fine, but why didn't you get a B." If the "B's" are obtained, "the B was good, but why didn't you get an A." Finally the child reaches the top of the heap and achieves an "A." Now the parent says, "that's great, but why didn't you do this before?" The child can't win - the standards are always the same, out of reach, and always signal a feeling of failure and defeat.

Perfectionism demands procrastination, because it defines the goal as the unattainable, therefore mandating failure. When the pursuit of excellence is associated with the feeling of failure, it will necessarily be avoided.

As an adult, the perfectionist uses a common strategy to avoid this feeling of failure. He puts off a task until the last minute, and then in a flurry of activity completes the task. Now the perfectionist has a perfect excuse. The accomplishment may be less than perfect, but after all, he only had a short time to do it. He unconsciously realizes that if he ever devotes his full effort to an activity, it will still not measure up to his standards. The consequent feeling of failure must be avoided at all costs to protect self-esteem. He scrupulously avoids giving his full effort to any task to avoid that feeling of failure, and procrastination is the perfect method.

## The Superman Syndrome

The Superman Syndrome is typified by an individual's attempt to establish superiority over other people. He boasts, brags, exaggerates, and inflates his self-worth to astonishing proportions. He constantly exalts his great achievements of the past and boasts of his marvelous plans for the future. But his accomplishment in the present is always lacking. He has such a compulsive need to avoid his fears of inferiority, he overinflates his self-worth to compensate. He's not content to be good, he must be great! He has unshakeable faith in his ability to master any area of endeavor. Unconsciously, he is aware that he is probably not of divine origin, and secretly fears to put his ability to the test and be found wanting. His method is simple; brag all you want, but avoid the performance. When performance is unavoidable, make sure you have plenty of excuses. You can see that procrastination is an invaluable implement in Superman's tool chest. He is very fond of the *Perpetual Preparation Strategy* described earlier.

Since he portrays himself as a person of superior

capacity and ability, he frequently bites off more than he can chew. It is not uncommon for Superman to become inundated by responsibility demands and time conflicts. To handle these problems, he applies heavy doses of procrastination until they go away. After a while, even his more ardent supporters cannot fail to notice the faded uniform and tarnished trophies, and simply quit believing him.

## HOW TO PUT OFF PROCRASTINATION

*Recognition and Reason*

One of the first methods for putting off procrastination is to simply recognize the reason behind the procrastination. In reading the causes of procrastination that have been described, you may find that you recognize yourself in one or more places. When you procrastinate again, if you will simply take a moment to become aware of the reason that you are procrastinating, you may then reason with yourself as to whether or not you choose to continue to deal with the situation in that manner. The simple recognition of motive and subjecting that motive to reason, will frequently liberate new found energy that will permit you to put off procrastination.

*Listen to Your Internal Dialogue*

Putting off procrastination is helped by becoming aware of how you talk to yourself. You may be creating passive-aggression in your behavior by subjecting yourself to a barrage of self-complaint. If you talk to yourself all day long in ridiculing, humiliating, shaming, condemning words, you will resist through procrastination just as you did as a child. Learn to be forgiving, gentle and tolerant with yourself and talk to yourself in the same understanding manner that you would use to coax an employee into an improved performance.

## *Emphasize Freedom of Choice*

People procrastinate because of too much pressure. They're given the feeling that they don't have any choice and to protect their autonomy, they procrastinate. Learn to emphasize your freedom of choice by never telling yourself that you have to do something. You don't have to do anything but die. The old adage that "you only have to die and pay taxes," isn't even correct because you don't have to pay taxes. Oh, it's true, you may go to jail, but you don't have to pay taxes. The reason that we do a thing is not because we have to, but because we choose to avoid the consequences of not doing it. In emphasizing freedom of choice, emphasize the consequences of a behavior, instead of the action of a behavior. To get by the barrier of procrastination, emphasize the way you will feel upon completing a task. Instead of haranguing yourself about having to complete it, avoid words like "should," "ought," "must," and "have to," and emphasize words like, "it's time to," or "I get to." Very few people procrastinate about having a good time, because nobody ever tells you that you have to have a good time. But we pressure ourselves to do productive work. "I have to go to work," "I ought to get to work now," "I must work today" all produce a pressure that demands procrastination. Permit yourself to work. Permit yourself to be successful. Tell yourself it's time to do something instead of you have to do something. It's marvelous that in this country of ours you get to go to a job and earn whatever your productivity will permit and be as successful as you choose. Emphasize your freedom of choice, and you will put off procrastination.

A final point in freedom of choice is that it's important to emphasize that you don't have to be successful. You can choose to be unsuccessful and that's your decision. Nobody can stop you from being a failure if that's what you want to do. So be clear on the fact that it's strictly choice and the choice is yours.

### Don't Master the Magnificent - Rule the Routine

As indicated, some people procrastinate because they set unattainable goals for themselves. Set smaller attainable tasks that emphasize the routine of behavior, instead of magnificent accomplishment. For instance, you may not be able to write a best seller, but you can complete a book. Or perhaps you feel you can't complete a book, but you could make an outline. Break the task down into its smallest component parts and take one step at a time. Rule the routine. You may not make a million dollars in real estate, but you could go to work on time and call 10 people today. When your goals are small enough to be attainable, you can leave at the end of each day feeling successful. When you constantly set goals that are magnificent in scope, they may be fine for cocktail party gossip, but they will increase your potential to procrastinate. If you learn to rule the routine, you will certainly master the magnificent.

### Examine Your Expectations

In keeping with the concept of ruling the routine, take a long hard look at what you are expecting of yourself. Make sure that your expectations are realistic and attainable. Are you setting goals for yourself that demand procrastination because they're unattainable? Your goals must be consistent with your ability, experience and circumstances. It will be far better for you to have a realistic income goal of $40,000 a year and attain that year after year, than to demand of yourself that you make a

$100,000 in a year and never make as much as $15,000 because of procrastination.

## Be Ready to Change Your Lifestyle

Don't wait until you achieve certain goals to change patterns of behavior. Start acting, thinking and living right now as a successful person. Gather friends around you and engage in behaviors consistent with the success that you desire. Think, act, and talk like the success that you desire and you will minimize procrastination from resistance to change.

## Emphasize Your Worth

Remind yourself daily that you will never be any more worthwhile than you are right now. Success will not make you worthwhile, it will simply produce a more enjoyable setting in which to appreciate your work. You do not work and achieve to be worthy, but because you're worthy. A dog doesn't bark to prove it's a dog, it barks because it's a dog. Emphasize your worth by remembering that success isn't something that you attain - success is something that you express. In conclusion, you can put things off and still be successful - as long as you put off procrastination!

*"Wisdom makes light the darkness of ignorance. As noble swans fly in the path of the sun, so the wise transcend this world."*

*Buddha*

The Enlightenment Amplifiers

ELLY LAROCQUE, D.D.
Box 257
Postal Station G
1075 Queen E.
Toronto, Ontario, M4M 3G7
(416) 465-4487

## ELLY LAROCQUE, D.D.

Dr. Elly Larocque is a writer, lecturer and ordained minister. Elly is the author of several short stories and articles, and is the executive director, pro-tem of National Speakers' Association of Canada, a non-profit organization being formed to offer recognition to Canadian speakers, the first of its kind in Canada.

Past President and Chairman of the Board of T.P.S.I., a three office private employment agency in Ohio, as well as Sales Manager, Elly is a licensed psychologist with an honorary Doctor of Divinity Degree from American Fellowship Church. Studies are in religious philosophy. Mother of three grown children and two grandchildren, she lives in Toronto, Canada with her husband, Mel.

Elly is conducting a scheduled tour across Canada and the United States on her favorite subject, "The Brain's Filing System."

POSITIVE

POWER

PEOPLE

The Enlightenment Amplifiers

# The Brain's Filing System Your Key To Enlightenment!

*By Elly Larocque, D.D.*

*"The sick are the greatest danger for the healthy: it is not from the strongest that harm comes to the strong, but from the weakest."*
*Nietzsche*

If someone told you they would share with you a scarcely known concept, which was the common denominator underlying most of the western world's problems, including, but not limited to, excessive tension, drinking problems, overweight, depression, shyness, neuroses, yes, and even some psychoses, - would you be interested? If so, you will want to hear my story, for I have such a secret!

If together we can open the channels of communication, so that you might practically comprehend my real meaning, I shall happily share this secret with you.

*Positive Thinking Not Enough*

I was a practicing positive thinker who fell prey to a king-sized hang-up which spiralled me into a nine year tailspin. Positive thinking, alone, I found, great as it is, is not enough. Just as the body, in order to feel in perfect health, must get rid of the common cold, so it is necessary to define and eliminate the snags in our psyches, before we can hope to achieve success and happiness in its highest measure.

*It is Not What Happens To Us, But How We React, That Is Important*

So say Hans Selye, Canadian stress expert, with great wisdom. In 1969 I was President and Chairman of the Board of my own private employment agency in Ohio. Two offices were flourishing, a third newly started, and a plan for franchising in the works when my troubles swelled to gigantic proportions.

The seeds of my demise, like the seeds of my success had been planted in my personality. Just as yours are, for good or bad, depending upon what has been sown as a result of your experiences.

In that one year, I experienced the staggering blows of my son's too hasty marriage, that same son's death, and the break-up of my own long standing marriage. As if that weren't enough in what seemed, "it never rains, but it pours," fashion, two thrashing, anti-establishment teens suddenly emerged from the chrysalis that had held staunch, loving children. And lastly, there was an automobile accident, when I was hit from behind by a Cola truck one slippery morning.

Like the driver of a kiddy car, hurtling downhill on a one way street in the wrong direction, I began to feel as if danger could threaten from anywhere and everywhere! Creditors soon became a problem as I reeled under each new blow and neglected essentials. An accelerated Charlie Chaplin film of something like "Poor Little Fool" might have been descriptive of my life that year. I sold my business for next to nothing and moved away.

## *Positive Thinker Wears Blinkers*

Yes, it isn't what happens to us that is important, only how we react. I had what it takes. I would build anew. I was still thinking positively. Unfortunately, I was not thinking correctly. I still had on my blinkers. The incredible thing about blinkers is that, until you get them off, you don't know you had them on! I couldn't see that I was causing many of my own problems in an orgy of ignorance.

If your soul isn't soaring...soaring, mind you, maybe you're wearing blinkers too. If we connect, and I hope we do, they'll disappear!

## *Power of Enlightenment*

A torticollis, or wry neck, became the outward manifestation of my acquired tension, which X-rays disclosed led to the deterioration of two neck discs. My biggest anxiety now, came from the embarrassment of not being able to keep my head still without holding it! I had acquired a king sized tension hang-up which led to loss of self esteem.

The principles by which I cured these problems, through the power of enlightenment which entered my life in a laser beam ray of conviction that I was completely well, is the secret I wish to share with you. Those same principles are completely workable for ALL OTHER HANG-UPS, INCLUDING YOURS, IF YOU HAVE ONE! And believe me, you are rare if you don't in our society today! The principles of which I speak are the physiological, seemingly miraculous phenomena lying behind Ziggy Ziglar's statement, "Humans were engineered to survive, designed to succeed."

*Computer Error...Error...Check Your Premise*

My mother diagnosed my condition as "nervous breakdown," and prescribed a long rest, with an obvious eye to picking up the pieces. Being alone felt more comfortable. Solicitude made me nervous, as did the company of my children. As for thoughts of my husband...I pushed them out of my head, convinced he had permanently damaged my neck during a quarrel. I positively thought, and would have no other thoughts before me.

Perhaps you, as I was, are convinced you know what is in your own head...my justification for not consulting an analyst. Besides, as a recently licensed psychologist, I shunned the idea of seeing a psychiatrist. But let me repeat, if you have a problem, try "listening" to your own thoughts. Put a friendly monitor on what you're telling yourself! You may be surprised, as I was when I finally realized my daily message to myself was that I must have been damaged. How was that for underestimating the curative powers of the body, and setting up just the right conditions to "act" damaged, because that was the message my central control tower was getting! But there's a price tag - an open mind - the willingness to admit maybe you've been wrong.

*Change of Pace*

Perhaps it was only natural, (and a bit lucky) that a positive thinker should find herself a new husband. He is quiet, calm, steady and understanding, a quiet lake, instead of a vibrant, crashing ocean. So soothing to jangled nerves. Best of all, our premises matched. Nine years slipped away before I realized I was hiding.

An ever widening gap existed between the successful executive I considered myself beneath my nervousness, and the middle-aged housewife I had become. True, the years had been somewhat productive. I wrote, became an ordained minister with an honorary Doctor of Divinity Degree, and even opened a small agency, but was forced to close it after a year. Spasmodic research, in psychology and religious philosophy seemed all that was left for me, because of the three day tension headaches, the high blood pressure, edema, and insipient diabetes. I was useless, or seemed so to myself. Even a part-time job seemed more than that with which I could cope.

I stood beside my kitchen stove one morning and was overcome by an agony of despair. I suddenly realized I was slowly but steadily slipping behind, physically and mentally.

*Prayer, The Beginning of Enlightenment*

A feeling of horrible anger at all who had injured me and a horror that I would never be any better shook me. Who was I kidding anyway? I wept for myself, for the nothingness I had become, in my own eyes. There seemed no place to turn. No point in living...

And then I prayed. I stormed and pleaded with Heaven in one final, desperate attempt for help. If there really is a God...if You can create miracles, if You really do care about people...about me...please, please help me! Make me calm, functional...I've done everything I can think of...I have never given up in all this time...until now...

A bargain! Use me! Do whatever You want with me, only cure me! Make me useful! Let me be whatever You want...

What is prayer to a Supreme Being, but the deep needs of humans seeking helpful information, input data, like a mini-computer connecting to a Great Terminal where all the answers are?

Shortly afterwards, my cure began. My perception sees this as cause and effect, but even if this were not so, and my perception somehow coloured, the chance of finding a cure AT JUST THAT TIME, AFTER NINE YEARS OF FAILURE TO DO SO...seems to me, astronomical.

*Where I Found My Secret*

The next day I was in the library doing research when I caught sight of a title. As soon as I saw it I knew it was significant..."Desuggestion", by E. Tietjens. It took me one year to digest that technical material into my own frame of reference to the point where I had the practical application of the author's message.

Because it has helped me, and others, I feel the import and impact of his findings for other humans is so mighty, that I take it as my duty to bring his work into the light. In addition, studies and empirical observations of my own based on both Tietjens and Wm. Godwin's writing, have resulted in the deceptively simple new concepts which follow. Such discoveries belong to everyone, and should not be hidden away in the "big word mystique" surrounding most psychological tenets.

*Not Generally Known to Professionals*

Recently I questioned a criminal psychologist speaking at a Gan-On meeting in Toronto, Canada, regarding the common denominator underlying neuroses and psychoses. His reply was that if he had that information he would be a millionaire! Yet that information will be made available to you in the following paragraphs!

In my book, THE BRAIN'S FILING SYSTEM, YOUR KEY TO HEAVEN ON EARTH,° N.S.A.C., supporting evidence is spelled out in detail. There is no room here for such elucidation, yet the essentials of this new concept, deceptively simple, are contained below.

## Excerpts From My Book

The term, emotional illness, like its predecessor, mental illness, is a misnomer, there being no such thing. The emotions are working very well, thank you, although overtime to be sure. And the mental processes, as well, are in good order, just as the Creator intended them to be.

## Common Denominator Underlying All Hang-ups

If all of the western world's "unhappiness" problems stem from a common denominator, what is it? The problem is, INCORRECT DATA, FED INTO THE FILING SYSTEM OF THE BRAIN, WHICH ACCEPTS WHAT IT IS GIVEN AS A VALID PREMISE ON WHICH TO ACT!

It is this, and this alone, which accounts for the bizarre, and seemingly "bad" behavior of the world, as well as annoying, and/or embarrassing inappropriate responses and success inhibitors, e.g. personality problems of shyness, excessive tension and its various physiological problems, e.g. torticollis, fear of failure, even criminal acts, rape, etc.

These incorrect premises become the basic thought blocks, upon which are structured other data, which may be valid in itself, but because of the premise, or starting point, it is incorrect, and therefore, has an incorrect outcome. It is the data which dictates the action.

## How To Know If Your Premise Is Incorrect

One way to test the validity of your data is to ask yourself if other people are bothered by the same problem. If the answer is no, then you can be almost certain you are the victim of an incorrect premise, an error in thinking. If the error isn't discovered and recognized as such, it is once again stored in the memory banks of the subconscious, awaiting recall, WHEN IT WILL ONCE AGAIN BECOME THE PREMISE (BASIS) FOR FUTURE ACTION. AND SINCE THE PREMISE IS INCORRECT, THE FUTURE ACTION CANNOT HELP BUT BE SO, WHENEVER THAT PARTICU- LAR EXPERIENCE, OR CLOSELY SIMILAR EXPERIENCE COMES UP AGAIN FOR CONSIDER- ED ACTION!

Corrected data, on the other hand, coupled with positive thinking, results in success, happiness, maxi- mum productivity and great human achievement, as well as goodness, and economic prosperity.

*What Is Incorrect Data?*

Generally speaking, incorrect data might be classified according to three main categories:
1. Errors someone else has passed on to us.
2. Errors of society generally regarded as truth.
3. Errors of our own.
   a. improperly correlated data
   b. obsolete data

*Countless Premises*

Since people's psyches differ only in their premises, it should be readily understood there are countless numbers of individual premises. All premises could never be discussed or dealt with, yet the malfunctioning of our lives, not operating at maximum potential, is the result of nothing but these incorrect premises. Do you see then the enormous importance of examining and searching out your thoughts for the truth content of your basic beliefs?

In my case, the error I filed was my own, an incorrect

conclusion of being "damaged" based on "obvious" facts...(a quarrel, pain, deteriorating discs, my limited knowledge of pinched nerves, etc.) which turned out to be incorrect deductions, errors of thinking, faulty premises! In addition to that error, (remember I said the thoughts form a network?) I was getting lots of regular obsolete printouts of the fear of confrontation.

This is the way it works: Each experience we have in life is recorded and noted for its pleasure content, and duly filed accordingly. Whenever we have a later, similar experience, the conscious mind, WITHOUT ASKING, OR EVEN DESIRING THAT INFORMATION IS PRESENTED WITH ALL AVAILABLE DATA AND ACCOMPANYING FEELING ASSOCIATED WITH THAT KIND OF EXPERIENCE! In other words, we are given a complete printout of that experience, which rises from the subconscious where the memory is stored in the memory banks, and is now flashed on the screen of the conscious mind.

This fear of confrontation from my husband and children was deeply grooved in and each time I saw them the tension was beyond my coping ability since I had no idea I was angry at them! Instead, I thought my tension was because I was damaged. (My incorrect premise.) What problem are you trying to cure through an effort of will? Oversimplified advice...find your premise!

### Instant Cure

There are three factors capable of changing behavior!
1. The conviction of having corrected data. (Cognition)
2. Neglect of the incorrect premise. (We must avoid playing the old recording...)
3. Firmly grooving in the corrected premise. (Play the new recording, often, with feeling.)

There are also two preconditions necessary, as the

overture to the symphony which effects the cure:

1. There must be a real benefit coming if we lose the problem. If there is a compensating benefit in having the problem, no cure will be effected! (This is because humans were designed to seek pleasure and avoid pain. (No room here to enlarge upon this, but in my book it is well substantiated. Since we were so designed, it is good to seek pleasure. It is more than good. It is vital to thriving survival.

2. The second precondition is that one must be able to fully understand, not only theoretically, but practically, the material here presented. The leap from theory to practice requires reading more than once, or twice.

The cognition, or conviction we mentioned is the underlying reason for all "miracle cures." While it is an exciting phenomenon, it is a gift, not available to a few, but something the Creator designed into the human psyche, and therefore available to all. How it is done is information you now have in these pages! WHATEVER A PERSON BELIEVES, as a result of experiences they have had, (which, incidentally, is not through any fault of their own!) THAT PERSON WILL ACT IN WHAT-EVER FASHION THEY ARE FEELING AND BE-LIEVING! THEY ARE COMPELLED TO DO SO BECAUSE OF THEIR BASIC PREMISE! If they believe they are healed, they ARE healed. If they believe they are a hopeless drunk, (for whatever reason) THIS IS WHAT THEY WILL CARRY OUT IN THEIR ACTIONS. THE CONVICTION IS AN ORDER TO THE CENTRAL CONTROL TOWER OF THE MIND WHICH MERELY IMPLEMENTS THE APPROPRIATE RESPONSE!!!

While it is true that changing the premise is not as easy as just reading this material, but also encompasses finding the wrong premise, examining it for truth, and then grooving in the new idea that we made an error, it can be done. And with not nearly the difficulty we have been led to suppose!

In closing, please remember to examine all present experiences for their "here and now" content, realizing the thing you feared on one occasion was actually an isolated instance, and that feeling you feel is just a memory, a printout of the past experience! It was valid perception, way back when, but is now obsolete!

We guarantee that if this message is really understood, if it is repeated (or if you repeat any new thought) often enough, and if it is really believed, the new information, the new premise, will be acted upon. It cannot be otherwise, according to the Creator's design of the human psyche! It is the way you "learned" your problem in the first place.

*"Life is a pure flame, we live by an invisible sun within us."*

*Sir Thomas Browne*

*"Power is always gradually stealing away from the many to the few, because the few are more vigilant and consistent!"*

*Samuel Johnson*

The Enlightenment Amplifiers

CAROL LARSEN-DYSART
Potentials Unlimited
1659 Mills Street
Chula Vista, California 92010
(714) 421-8085    (714) 421-6468

## CAROL LARSEN-DYSART

Consultant * Trainer * Professional Speaker

Carol Larsen-Dysart, President and co-founder of Potentials Unlimited, a training and management consulting service, is a consultant in Human Relations, Communications Skills, Motivation and Work-Behavior Styles Analysis.

As a National Trainer for an in-depth personal development process known nationally as "Human Potential Seminar" (HPS) she coordinates and trains leaders to use the process in their field of interest or work.

As a Certified Consultant for Performax Systems, Inc., she delivers and interprets highly developed instruments which reveal persons' work and personal behavior styles, climate impact, accuracy of perception of job factors and attitudinal listening styles.

Mother of three children, Julie (16), Lori (10) and Scott (7), she successfully combines an active family life with her career demands. Interested in helping parents raise children to become self-confident and productive adults, she speaks and does workshops in this area, using a Child's Profile and analysis.

Carol's credentials include a B.A. in Education from UCLA and a Masters of Science in Counseling from San Diego State University. She teaches consulting and trainer certification courses for UCSD and is active in local chapters of A.S.T.D., Career Guidance Association, Personnel and Guidance Association, Career Woman's Association and California Association for the Gifted and

Talented.

Carol and her associates in Potentials Unlimited are available to lead seminars and workshops or speak at meetings or conventions on:
- Basic Human Potential Seminar (Empathy , Values, Motivators, and Goals)
- Advanced Human Potential Seminar (Conflict I.D., Management or Resolution, and Life Style Planning)
- Effective Communication Skills
- Stress Management
- Synergist Team Building
- Personal Profile System (Adult or child)
- Dealing with Failure Successfully
- Dealing with Criticism

POSITIVE
POWER
PEOPLE
*The Enlightenment Amplifiers*

*"Life is a mission. Religions, science, philosophy, though still at variance upon many points, all agree in this, that every existence is an aim."*
                    *Mazzini*

**POSITIVE**
**POWER**
**PEOPLE**
*The Enlightenment Amplifiers*

# Turning On The Power To Your Unlimited Potential

*By Carol Larsen-Dysart*

*"You and I possess within ourselves, at every moment of our lives, under all circumstances, the power to transform the quality of our lives."*
*Anonymous*

We are not the victims of circumstances. We are the architects of our entire life. I know you've heard this before. It is so easy to talk about it, but applying that understanding is not always so simple...or so it seems. But are you aware of the POWER you have to change your life? To make things happen the way YOU want them to?

What would you like? Close your eyes and dream a little

right now. Take a deep breath and think about one or two things you would really like to have, places you would like to go, achievements you would like to make your own, relationships you would choose if you could.

Do you have a business idea? Do you know how to promote it? Do you know where your resources for people, ideas and money are? Do you know what your ideal job or career would be if you could write the script? Knowing the answers to these questions could mean the difference between success and mediocrity. And which do YOU want?

What do you do when you are blocked? How assertive or creative can you be? Can you think "laterally" instead of linearly? Can you go around, over, under, or through your "block"?

Here is what I did when I was blocked from continuing in a career I knew I wanted.

I had loved my work as a high school and college teacher, a job I had for the first five years of married life. But because I was determined not to work full time once I had "little ones" at home, I resigned at the birth of my first child.

Though busy at home with the children, I found ways to keep alive my intense interest in the business world by participating in several entrepreneurial at-home business-es over the next seven years. This kept me in "pin money" and offered me contact with "real people". But I was anxious to get back to my teaching career as soon as the children went to school. So that I would be a more effective teacher, I completed a Masters degree in Counseling at night during those years at home. Alas, when I was finally ready to return to teaching, there were no job openings for teachers or counselors, and my seniority didn't count anymore. What to do?

My dilemma was intensified by the fact that I was in the process of divorce, and I knew I would need substantial income shortly. For several years I had realized that I was not the right mate for my husband. He wanted an "old fashioned wife," and that just wasn't ME! So we agreed to a compatible dissolution contract, requested joint custody for our children's sake, and filed our own divorce papers. Through open communication and expressing of our true needs to each other, we avoided the "typical" fault-finding games that many play, and as a result still count each other as friends.

Not wanting any job (or lack of one) to control my destiny, I merged talents with two friends who were also single parents and we formed a seminar business to help others who were lacking goal direction, stick-to-it-iveness and self esteem. We called our company POTENTIALS UNLIMITED for the unlimited potential within each of us. I'm sure we couldn't have fully realized the implications of that name when we chose it. Oh, we knew that we all do less than we might. But what wasn't clear was that we could demonstrate it in reading, memorizing, learning and meeting the demands of the "Knowledge Explosion" era we were in.

Taking a part-time consulting/teaching job with a learning-effectiveness company teaching speed reading, I began to catch a glimpse of the possibilities for academic excellence by anyone. It was wonderful to watch my own reading speed soar from a high of 350 words a minute to an unbelievable speed of 18,000 words a minute - and with a high comprehension!

What made the difference? How could I be accomplishing this in less than one week? My boss's approach to teaching was different than any I had ever known before. Daily preparation included regular readings of positive affirmations on being one of the greatest readers in the world, seeing myself enjoying reading as my fingers flew down the pages. I learned to teach others to change their attitudes about their own reading habits by thinking and concentrating on what they could do. ATTITUDES! This is what *my* business was all about.

While teaching, I saw readers reading so rapidly that turning the pages fast enough was the problem! Eight to twenty thousand words a minute was not unusual! It seemed incredible, yet the comprehension was extremely high. It was as if the words on the page reeled by like a movie on a screen and the reader was just there to watch! (This actually is what happens when the reader is prepared and relaxed.) My boss had been applying new learning methods which were developed by Dr. Georgi Lozanov in Bulgaria during the 60's. Lozanov found ways to integrate the "right side of the brain" - our intuitive creative side - with the "left side" - our linear, logical thinking side. With the proper environment and mental attitudes students were learning foreign languages in record time.

His method included the use of special background music that had a tempo and rhythm which closely matched the body's resting heartbeat...about 60 beats per minute. This was interesting! I must do some research!

In a book by Ostrander and Schroeder called "Superlearning" (Delacorte. Press/New York, 1979) I found much to confirm my hunches and to validate observations I had been making about my own ease of learning and its transferance to other areas of my life. Their report on research done on the mind/body approach to unlocking virtually limitless capacities of ourselves excited me. Lozanov was not an educator, but a doctor and psychiatrist who was interested in studying the nature of the human being in all its potential. He and other scientists spent many years in research backed by their government on the exploration of their country's "human resources".

They found that not only does one's body have to relax to take in more information, but for retention to be high, the mind must be alert and able to concentrate. Lozanov found that certain forms of music with specific, regular tempos could induce a relaxed state in the body that left the mind alert and able to concentrate. The heartbeat slows down and brain waves approach what is known as the alpha rhythm. The body and mind are now in harmony, and with the slower heartbeat, mind efficiency takes a quantum leap forward! *This* was why I felt so good in the morning when my clock radio woke me with Baroque-period music!

I had noticed a connection between music and learning efficiency myself during college, but hadn't realized the substance of my discovery. One evening, while preparing to study for an important final exam, I had been called to help usher at a concert given by the famous classical pianist, Leonard Pennario. What a decision! Should I stay and study the hours I knew it would take me, or go enjoy the concert and be of help? I decided to sacrifice some sleep and do both!

Afterwards, I felt uplifted by the exquisite performance of superb classical music I had just heard. I eagerly settled in to begin my studies, now three hours behind schedule.

To my surprise, I had such a sense of energy and concentration that I covered all the material in record time, got a good night's sleep, and got an "A" on the final...with "effortless effort." I remember thinking that it felt like my whole mind and body had been opened up during that musical experience, and my creative thinking had been amplified.

Throughout the next few years of my college career as a music education major, I noticed similar uplifting experiences when I performed in or attended concerts of great music. I also noticed an uncomfortable feeling when hearing dissonant 20th century composers with their irregular rhythm and clashing harmonies.

What I didn't realize then was that the only music that gives the harmonious mind/body consonance is the slow movements of 16th to 18th Century composers like Bach, Telemann, Handel, Corelli and Vivaldi. There seems to be a correlation to their 60 beat-per-minute tempo and the relaxed heartbeat!

What an interesting added dimension to my love of music, teaching and counseling this knowledge would bring! I learned that even playing this kind of music in the background of classroom presentations seems to open up the receptivity of the right brain and allows learning to take place faster and more easily. Just think of how exciting this information could be for teachers with students of any learning level!

Another thing about the Lozanov research and teaching method that intrigued me was that there is a new "joy in learning" with this approach. It recaptures that sense of exhilaration we had as a child when we learned new skills: how to walk, talk, tie a shoe. As adults, we get caught up in what could be called "the conspiracy against knowing who you are." New learning systems support self-discovery by providing a new environment for knowledge, free of tension, worry and boredom. Trying too hard only hampers our ability. Superlearning is stress-free and a pleasure. "Effortless effort!"

In a sense, superlearning adds by taking away. The programs are geared to help dissolve fear, self-blame, cramped self-images and negative suggestions about limited abilities. They try to flood away the many blocks we handicap ourselves with and release the unobstructed potential. The possibilities are limitless. What an unlimited potential we have! Potentials Unlimited. I was glad we had chosen that name.

The consulting and seminar business was picking up. Now I realized I would need more business development skills than I had received as an Education major in college. You can imagine my delight when I learned that a new business school had moved its headquarters to San Diego that was teaching Business through Superlearning principles! Their graduates seemed to be achieving phenomenal financial success by applying their newly discovered powers in memory, speed reading, relaxed learning and personal and business goal setting.

I wanted to see for myself, so I visited the Burklyn Business School in session. Here I observed 50 students not only surviving, but excelling in a curriculum that looked extremely ambitious to the outsider. Exercising by 7 a.m. and in classes that lasted from early morning to late at night for four weeks straight, these residential students expressed tremendous enthusiasm, energy and joy at all times. They were accomplishing in 90 minutes exercises that took Harvard Business students 2 1/2 days to complete! The difference from traditional learning environments was obvious to the observer. There was "special" music in the background during all classes - (they had brought Lozonov over to train them their first year in business) - they did special relaxation exercises throughout the day, breaks were taken every 50 minutes and often included mind agility games to keep everyone at peak performance. The founder of the school, Marshall Thurber, had applied learning, synergy principles and "fun" atmosphere to his multi-million dollar Real Estate business for three years and was now teaching these principles to eager men and women who were ready to make a positive change in business across the country. This was "effortless effort" applied to the maximum.

Learning and business could be fun!

The interesting thing is that these ideas for developing a "win/win" work climate can be applied anywhere...in the home, at the office, in our lives and relationships. We have all the joy, energy, creativity within ourselves already! Sometimes we need a little encouragement and a gentle nudge to prove it to ourselves. I like to think that we are like sunbeams, transmitting our light from the sun, our Source. We don't have to "get" anything to carry out our job or to be a better sunbeam. We only have to "be" what we are and let others see our light in us! It is already there for us to express. And we spend so much time and effort "hiding" it! Then we spend the rest of our time trying to "find" it! All we ever need to do is just "be" it. Then notice how all of our life "works".

Watching the positive attitude of the Burklyn group, I was reminded of a little-known fact that is worth remembering. Positive thoughts seem to create a chemical effect in the body which is very beneficial to our system. They have a healing effect on us more powerful than medicine. Negative thoughts, on the other hand, create a toxic chemical that is very damaging to the body. I remembered this when I read of an interview with a carpet cleaning specialist who commented that he could remove blood from a carpet IF it had been caused by a cut or an accident. But if it were from an act of violence, it was impossible to remove because of the chemicalization that occurred! "Wow" "Be careful of your thoughts", I said to myself!

In the Human Potential Seminar process I lead, part of the seminar develops awareness of the word patterns we use unthinkingly. "Which 'potential killers' do YOU tend to use most often?" is a question I pose after brainstorming all the negative word possibilities the group can think of. Some of the more popular 'killers' of our full use of our potential are: "I can't", "I won't", "It costs too much," "I don't have enough (time, money, energy, etc.)", "It hasn't been proven", "Later", and "No way".

Next, we become aware of how many 'potential helpers' we can choose to replace those. Words like, "I can," "I'll do it now," "After all, what's the worst possible thing that could happen?," "I'll make the (time, money, effort) available," "Why not?," etc. These words seem a little harder to think of, but the group helps each member replace negative talk with positive affirmations through-out the seminar, and then each member is encouraged to elicit the aid of someone close to him/her to continue to monitor their talk at home until the new positive habits are firmly established.

I believe firmly in the power of asking for help from others. I try to help others see that it is alright, in fact, advisable, to ask for support from others. Of course, it never hurts to give a little yourself too!

Some people are uncomfortable to learn that wherever they are right now in their life is exactly where they want to be! It takes a desire to change before new life styles are developed. "We walk in the direction in which we look" is certainly true for me. If I think happy and look for positive results, somehow things always turn out alright. This is not to say that I have never made mistakes. I have trusted others who have disappointed me or led me in the wrong direction for a time, but in retrospect, they also provided the lesson I needed to learn at that time. In my view, I have never had a failure; only temporary setbacks and experience that was valuable. To me, failure is only when you don't get back up after you are down!

I believe in hiring experts in areas where I am short on expertise, but experience is the one thing I have to get for myself. There is no consultant in the world at any price, who can give me the experience I get by trying things out, taking risks, and learning to trust my own judgement.

I'd like to share just how I have applied the principles I teach in my personal life recently, and I hasten to add that, while it looks and sounds like a fairy tale, it did happen. It is exciting and encouraging to know that these principles do work.

After I had been single for over four years, my new husband and I fell in love the day we met. Interestingly enough, it was only two weeks after I had become very aware and clear that I was very happy being single. I thought, "If I do re-marry, it will be with the perfect right partner who already exists and is ready for me to come into his life!"

I made a list of all the qualities I desired and would require when he showed up: honesty, integrity, sense of humor, high spiritual consciousness and intelligence. I wanted him to be a lover of children (especially mine!), well educated, culturally well-rounded, interested in creative business enterprises, enthusiastic and optomistic about life in general, and supportive of a moving, growing continually changing lifestyle. I also affirmed that he would be tall, dark and handsome and be a great dancer! (I didn't want much!)

I knew that the first step in effective affirmations is to visualize exactly what you want. But the next step is the one most people leave out. You have to behave as if you already have what you want. In my case, I needed to express the qualities I desired, myself, to everyone in my life. I knew that only by demonstrating the qualities I desired would I attract someone who also expressed, and therefore recognized, those qualities in me!

The power of this awareness and application was dramatic. I started "being" all the things on my list and really enjoying being single. After our first date, it was only a matter of a short time before we were sure we wanted to be married...and he had all of the requirements on my list! "Effortless effort."

We both recognize and acknowledge the power within us to create the kind of life and relationship we desire. Between us we have three children, Tom's daughter, Julie (16), has emerged like a positive, beautiful butterfly out of a negative cocoon of self doubt into a radiant young adult who is proud of her talents. My daughter Lori, (10), and son Scott (7), keep us on our toes and do most of the "teaching" in our family. "Here is what I appreciate about you" is a favorite family game that has helped establish harmony instead of friction many times. We are teaching the children that they don't have to give their power away to anyone or any incident unthinkingly. They can take responsibility for their own feelings, share them, and keep control of the situation.

Power cannot be taken away from us if we don't give it

away. If we "let the resistance (of life) go by us", we keep our center and are able to withstand all the elements that would pull or push us down. I am learning to trust myself, to let my inner voice give me right answers. I make few mistakes when I really listen to the Father for direction, and I am thrilled to see this understanding in my own children. One day Lori said to me, "Mommy, when I listen to my thoughts, they always give me the right answers. The other day I didn't listen to them and I did the wrong thing. I realized it would have been better to do what my mind was telling me!"

What a wonderful power for her to discover at this early age!

She has the basis for true self-esteem - the ability to trust in self. There are few problems in life that cannot be solved with love, empathy and understanding. As I work with others who desire to be workshop leaders in the "HPS" process, a positive experimental chance to discover what is "right" with one, I see that most all "problems" stem from the need for acknowledgment. No matter what the "story" about the problem is, the underlying feeling of longing, hurting, fearing all comes from the need for someone else to tune into and acknowledge what is "right".

We all need acknowledgment. I try to acknowledge all the people in my life as often as possible. "HAVE YOU HUGGED YOUR KID TODAY?" is my favorite bumper sticker. We forget to give each other the strokes, the compliments, the nurturing and loving support that releases those positive chemicals in the body, gives inspiration and allows further exploration of our unlimited potentials.

A dear friend of ten years gave me this sign to post on my bulletin board, "P.M.A. in all that you do". Positive Mental Attitude. It really works because our mental attitude is the filter through which we perceive everything that happens in our personal world. Our brain can only focus on one stimuli at a time - positive or negative. It is our choice at all times to flinch at the bitterness of the lemon or to make lemonade!

All the success books come back to one principle: whatever your consistent expectations are, whatever you dream, that is what you will achieve, if you set action goals around them and KEEP TRYING. We must think positively about ourselves. After all, if we don't how can we expect others to?

Blocks? They are only temporary interruptions and a chance to learn a lesson. Laterally think around those setbacks. Tune into your Source. Listen. Feel. Hear the dynamic vibrations, the ringing patterns of the universal power that is there for all to tune in on at all times. I like to think of my mind as a radio, tuning in on the station of my choice. If I am tuned completely off the station, I get nothing but static. If I am tuned just slightly off the mark, I get a fuzzy reception. But when I am focused right on the channel, the messages and music come through loud and clear! When I turn off my receiver, I cannot hear any messages, even though the broadcast is still going on. It is nice to know that I can always turn it back on and start receiving the benefits of the program at any time.

That is our choice at all times. Transform the quality of YOUR life right now! You have unlimited potential and YOU ARE A WINNER!

The Enlightenment Amplifiers

PAUL P. TALBOT
Paul Talbot and Associates, Inc.
308-698 Seymour Street
Vancouver, B.C. Canada V6B3K6
(604) 689-8985

## PAUL P. TALBOT

Paul Talbot is a specialist in PERSONNEL CONSULT-
ING, OFFICE/WORD PROCESSING SYSTEMS
CONSULTING and EDUCATIONAL TRAINING. He
is President of PAUL TALBOT & ASSOCIATES INC.,
Personnel Consultants, Director/Trainer of TEELINE
EDUCATIONAL SERVICES (B.C.) LTD., Consultant
of WORD PROCESSING PERSONNEL and Director/
Consultant of ALL ABOUT WORD PROCESSING,
INC.

**WORK EXPERIENCE INCLUDES:**
Consultant/Trainer of secretarial and word processing
Co-author, trainer and director of TEELINE shorthand.
Business Education Instructor of secretarial subjects
(including word processing) for Vancouver Vocational
Institute, Vancouver Community College.
Community Education Services instructor of the
Vancouver School Board and Vancouver Community
College.
Office Manager, Vancouver law office.
Private Secretary/Personal Assistant, London, England
and Tripoli, Libya.

**EDUCATION:**
Instructor's Diploma, "COMMERCE" University of
B.C.
Professional Standards Diploma, "EDUCATION
Advanced".
National Association for Educational Secretaries.
Granted "ASCT" by the Society of Commercial Teachers,
London, England.
Several diplomas and certificates in "COMMERCE",
"EFFECTIVE      COMMUNICATION"      and
"PERSONNEL PRACTICES".

POSITIVE

POWER

PEOPLE

*The Enlightenment Amplifiers*

# "Stop Whining and Start Winning"

*By Paul P. Talbot*

*"Our greatest glory consists not in never falling, but in rising every time we fall. Whatever you do, you need courage. Whatever course you decide upon, there is always someone to tell you you are wrong. There are always difficulties arising which tempt you to believe that your critics are right. To map out a course of action and follow it to an end requires some of the same courage which a soldier needs. Peace has its victories, but it takes brave men to win them. Make the most of yourself, for that is all there is to you.*
　　　　　　　*Ralph Waldo Emerson*

Life is what you make it - so start now!

How true, we can be what we want to be but first we must know what we want, how to get it is another matter. You have to want it so badly that you think, sleep and feel it - that's where I've been, and it's getting better all the time.

Not being a car driver I travel all the time on public transport and so often I sit back and smile at what I am hearing - was I once like that? People complain about their job, friends and life and yet they do very little or nothing about it - why? Is it because they are in that comfortable rut with job security (of one kind or another) or is it because that BIG step, that gamble in life in DOING SOMETHING is too big to take? Making a decision of any kind is difficult nowadays, but to change your career path and go off into another direction, boy that takes guts and perhaps you have to be a little crazy to do it - I've certainly done that!

Thinking back I've always been adventurous and aiming for the stars (perhaps a dreamer, but always searching). Being the eldest of seven, four sisters and two brothers, I guess I had to set an example - we were and are still very close. We grew up sharing, we never went without, and often wonder now how our parents did it. I was the first and only one to leave home, unheard of at that time, but I did it, I was searching.

My childhood was normal, schooling average, and when I left school I undertook business training - this included shorthand and typing, both of them carried me into high paying positions. At that time I typed 90 words per minute on a MANUAL typewriter and shorthand of 140 - in those days you were expected to do more than your best, training for which I am thankful.

I drifted into my youth (not job to job) but unsure in my mind what I wanted to do, no goals but waiting for the right time to make a move and a DECISION. I did! I left home and moved to the big city, London, England. First time away from home and unsure of myself. However, I soon found work and somewhere to live. I decided at this time to continue my education and quickly enrolled in an evening program for Business Administration. To this day I firmly believe that continuing education for all ages is vital.

## Opportunity Calls

The company I was working for at the time (I was in the accounting dept.) put out an urgent call asking for someone with shorthand and typing to report to personnel (this due to a flu epidemic at the time) within minutes I was working as Secretary to the Vice-President of Marketing. After I finished my assignment, and the regular secretary returned, my boss called me to one side and suggested that I pursue a career as a "secretary". That evening I looked through the papers and was amazed at the number of openings for "male secretaries". In just a short while I was now taking another stepping stone in my life - as a secretary!

I was lucky, I'm a good organizer and am blessed with a good memory. Starting out as trainee stenographer I soon climbed the ladder to Private Secretary to a multi millionaire dealing in real estate and office blocks. My boss had a temper, my spelling was not the greatest and the word "no" was a word that you did not use. Once I had a special project to complete but I already had something in my typewriter (manual typewriter as well) and he wanted a 'rush' letter typed - within seconds he had another machine delivered so as not to upset the production line. I soon learned how to cope with his massive files and control the workloads. Although the going at first was rough it was a question of "sink or swim".

The knowledge and information I gained with this man has put me in good stead and I thank him many many times for the training I obtained. It also made me realize that I could do ANYTHING and that I could do it by using my secretarial skills. I wanted to be successful - this of course means different things to us all. My secretarial career then took me to Tripoli, Libya where I worked for the Project Manager of an American oil company. Excitement, pressure and exhilaration were just part of the job and what I was feeling. My parents were so proud and so was I. Afterall, I had been chosen from a list of over 30 applicants.


## There Was No Stopping, No Turning Back

Returning to England, I had the wanderlust - having relatives in Canada I decided to visit. Playing it safe I applied for immigration and within two weeks of arriving was working in the accounting department of a large law firm. Within six months I was made office manager. I was able to use my shorthand and typing in the job but male secretaries were few and far between on the West Coast, I was like a square peg in a round hole - so I had to compromise, for a while, and I did.

For 18 months I enjoyed the work and again I was taking evening courses, after all, I was a foreigner and had to master new customs. One day a friend said to me, "With your secretarial skills and working background you should go into teaching." Six months later I was a teacher. Back to University (part time and during the summer months) I was carrying a full teaching load and there I stayed at Vancouver Community College for seven years. I presently still teach part time for the college. During this time I obtained a teaching degree for Commerce in the public school system.

Yet again I was to close a door and open another - not sure as to the 'why' but just knowing it was something I had to do.


## The Doors Open

My decision to leave the College was a sudden one. Although doubts in my mind as to what I wanted to do kept cropping up, I was not happy but I was not unhappy, I just felt unrest.

I did all the things that the experts tell you NOT to do. No goals written down, no discussion with friends or bank managers, I just knew I was going to START MY OWN BUSINESS. I like people and with good secretarial skills, the answer seemed to be a personnel agency and secretarial services. PAUL TALBOT & ASSOCIATES, Inc. was born. We are Personnel/Management Consultants and offer Secretarial/Word Processing Services.

When I look back at the ups and downs in my life and at the four years in business for myself I often think "why!" Guts, pride and determination kept me going and still do!

During this time I formed a shorthand company and co-authored the Canadian edition of TEELINE shorthand as well as conducting seminars and teaching in the evenings. Time management is what I practice. A "must" for anyone in business for themselves. After all, time is money.

I've always been involved and of course, belong to many professional organizations. At present, I am the only male member in Canada for the National Secretaries Association (International) - again, another round peg in a square hole but this organization has helped me grow. I could have sat back and been 'just a member' but with both feet in I fell, and was soon chairing committees and speaking to groups. The involvement, people and contacts enhanced my business and along the way I made many new friends - friends I could turn to for help or advice, they were there when the going got rough when I needed someone to talk to. Remember, friends are rare, don't lose touch with them.

In the early days there was just me, now there is a staff of seven and we recently opened our first branch office.

Owning your own business is not easy but it is rewarding and satisfying. There are no short cuts, no magic words just hard work. If you are thinking about opening your own business - do it! Otherwise this nagging feeling will continue until you do.

My home life, education and career path have been 'average' no silver spoons in my mouth, no sudden inheritance. Just the need to do something with my life, that makes me happy, that makes me tick. I've gotten out of the rut - I've stopped whining and I'm now a winner - you too can be one.

GOOD LUCK!

*"Give me a lever long enough, and fulcrum strong enough, and single handed I have the power to move the world.*

*Archimedes*

The Enlightenment Amplifiers

JAN L. GAULT, Ph.D.
Uptime
55 New Montgomery, Suite 305
San Francisco, CA 94105
(415) 957-1774

## JAN L. GAULT, Ph.D.

Jan L. Gault, Ph.D. is the founder and director of Uptime, a San Francisco based firm specializing in personal growth and success through creative and leisure time management. Through seminars, lectures and individual consultations, Dr. Gault has helped hundreds of people to lead more meaningful and successful lives.

She is publisher and editor of "Leisure Power", a newsletter which provides practical suggestions, feature articles and guidelines for success to thousands of readers.

Jan Gault has had over five years experience as an educator and instructor in Honolulu where she developed and taught courses in social psychology, personality and creativity. A former instructor of human development at the University of Hawaii, Dr. Gault has done extensive research in personality, leisure behavior and time management.

She is presently active in many San Francisco Bay Area organizations and is a member of World Future Society, Think Tank Unlimited, Toastmistress and National Speakers Association.

Dr. Gault has been featured on major radio and television networks and media throughout the United States, Canada and Australia and is author of the book, Leisure...Your Way to Success.

POSITIVE

POWER

PEOPLE

*The Enlightenment Amplifiers*

# LEISURE POWER

*By Jan L. Gault, Ph.D.*

*"The advantage of leisure is mainly that we may have the power of choosing our own work, not certainly that it confers any privilege of idleness."*
    *John Lubbock [Lord Avebury]*
    *The Pleasure of Life VI*

"How did you ever get into the leisure business - you're one of the busiest persons I know?" is a question I am frequently asked as founder and director of Uptime, a leisure consulting firm in San Francisco.

Too often leisure is equated with laziness, as being laid back, loafing or even sinfulness. Nothing could be further from the truth.

### Leisure as Choice

Leisure has to do with our freedom. Within the context of time, "leisure" is the free part of that space - the space where we have the possibility of choice. As such, what we do in our leisure (those hours when we are freest to be ourselves) tells a lot about who we are and the direction in which we're headed.

One way to think about leisure is as a "raw commodity" or a "potential" to shape and mold according to our hopes, aspirations and dreams. It can be a time for personal growth, to tap our creativity, improve our relationships or to achieve greater financial independence. The choice is ours.

## Funny How Time Gets Away

"Ah, that is all very fine", you protest, "Sure, I know a lot of things I would like to do, but when? I never seem to have enough time."

Traditionally leisure has been thought of as time left over after work and obligations. But work in a sense is NEVER done - whether you have a 9 - to - 5 job, are in business for yourself, in sales or even unemployed. There is always work to be done and a seemingly endless stream of demands, pressures and obligations. We never quite get "caught up". And this can leave us feeling frustrated, anxious and guilty. WHERE is the leisure?

## Dare to TAKE Time

One of the most important lessons I learned was many years ago as a housewife and mother living in a small town in the Midwest. I had had a particularly hectic day. The dryer broke and I was down to the baby's last diaper. It was a chilling December day and as I hung them out on the line to dry, they were freezing almost as fast as I could put them up. Chuck, my three year old, who is presently an artist, was demonstrating his talents even then by decorating the bedroom walls with glowing colored crayons. Laura, my little girl, had picked that day to lose herself in the hallway closet peacefully napping while I frantically searched the neighborhood for her.

At the end of the day, I collapsed on the sofa, my thoughts churning about all the things that still needed to be done. Bridge club was meeting tonight, I had to shower, wash my hair, press clothes and then find time to bake the dessert I had so readily VOLUNTEERED to do. It would be nice to just stay home, curl up and read a good book. I loved to read but there never seemed to be any time lately. I picked up a magazine and lazily flipped through the pages. An ad caught my eye: "WIN a trip to Europe and dozens of other prizes. Send your entry in today."

I sighed. Even if I won a trip to Europe, I wouldn't have time to go. Nevertheless, as I continued to read about the contest, I became intrigued. SOMEONE must be winning all those contests. Wouldn't it be fun to enter and actually win something. The competition must be fierce. What a challenge!

The phone rang. It was my friend, Pat, reminding me that she would be picking me up in an hour for bridge club. I made a quick decision.

"I'm not going", I told her. I had been playing bridge for years and although I initially found it stimulating, lately I'd had to push myself to go. Mostly, I realized, I had continued to go simply out of habit. I hung up the phone, called someone to substitute for me and put on my coat to pick up some brownies at the store to drop off for the club.

When I got back home I felt a sense of relief. How many other things had I been doing just out of habit or as a response to pressures from others? I vowed to reassess the events in my life. Many times I would have preferred to just be alone and take some time for myself. Did I feel guilty just taking time for me? Perhaps. I picked up a pencil and paper and jotted down some figures. If I took only 30 minutes a day - over a year that would amount to

182 HOURS, or more than 4 - 40 hour weeks! That's a lot of time. I made the decision not to feel guilty about taking 30 minutes a day just for myself - NO MATTER HOW MUCH WORK WAS LEFT UNDONE.

*Do What YOU Want To Do...Not What Others Think You Should Be Doing*

I picked up the contest blank again and read the rules. Entries would be judged according to creativity, appropriateness and clarity. You could use no more than 50 words. It was a national contest and entries were expected to run in the millions. The thought of my entry making its way through all those other contestants' entries and coming out a winner fascinated me. I decided to give it a try.

The next day after mailing in my "brainchild", I enthusiastically called up Pat to tell her about it.

"What?" she exclaimed, "Jan, DON'T YOU KNOW all contests are fixed? You have to know someone to win anything. I've never heard of ANYONE winning."

Other friends, relatives and acquaintances concurred and were quick to tell me, "What a foolish way to spend your time. Contests are all based on chance and luck. I thought you were brighter than that."

Now I've never been a lucky person. In a sweepstakes drawing with only two entries I'd be the loser. But I am a trusting person. I did not believe for a minute that all contests were fixed nor that winning was based strictly on chance. If the rules said "creativity counted 65%, appropriateness 20% and clarity 15% in the selection of winners" then it seemed to me all I had to do was figure out exactly what that meant and do it. As far as I was concerned it depended mostly on me and my ability.

I'm also stubborn and not easily intimidated by others' ideas of what I should be doing. I was more determined than ever.

I began seeking out contests and found that I could often create entries in my head as I went about my household chores of dishes, making beds and cleaning.

Before I knew it, prizes were starting to roll in...an electric blanket, a 14K gold-and-cultured-pearl bracelet, a new wardrobe, cameras, elegant dinners, trips and CASH. Nearly every week I would receive a phone call or a letter that started off with "CONGRATULATIONS... YOU HAVE WON..."

## How To Win

You may not be interested in spending your spare time entering contests - nor would I recommend it in today's market - but the same principles hold true wherever your interests lie.

Before I even picked up a pencil to write down the winning entry, I tried to find out everything I could about the sponsor's service or product. What was unique and special about it? What were the positive features and how did it differ from its competitor's products? I studied the ads and tried out the products. But more than that, I BELIEVED IT WAS POSSIBLE TO WIN AND TO WIN CONSISTENTLY. My encouragement and reinforcement came from within and sparked my enthusiasm to write interesting and winning entries.

Whether you are trying to make a sale, get a raise from your employer or win over a lover, by focusing on their special qualities, being genuinely interested and believing that you can do it will put you on top.

Writing entries provided a creative outlet that took minimal time and could be done along with other routine chores. Often many of the perfunctory but necessary tasks in our lives can be combined with more challenging and stimulating activities.

*Check Out Your Leisure*

Begin by taking stock. Keep track of your time for a few days. My clients make use of a Time Reactor Log (TRL) where they log in every few hours exactly what they have been doing and how they are reacting to the events of the day. Writing down your activities will raise your awareness of the way you spend your time and how this relates to your goals and your enjoyment. You find out exactly where your time is going. It is one thing to feel that time is getting away from you, but quite another to know - to see logged in precisely where the minutes and hours are going.

Making the effort to keep track of your time for a few days will be well worth it. You will become more conscious of how you are spending your time and some of the habits that you have gotten into that are no longer consistent with your objectives.

Next, ask yourself, "What leisure activities and events in your life are fun, rewarding, stimulating or satisfying?" Plays, reading, jogging, conversations with friends, swimming, hot air ballooning...the list is endless. Then take a look at the kinds of activities where you are spending the bulk of your time. Social scientists have found that there is often an inverse relationship between what we do in our leisure and what we enjoy doing. That is, we may be participating in a lot of activities that we do not especially enjoy, or conversely, not doing a lot of things that we would find very satisfying and rewarding.

Not infrequently a client will tell me that his or her favorite leisure pastime is something such as swimming, playing a musical instrument or tennis but it may have been weeks, months or even years since they last did it.

Americans spend over $160 billion a year on leisure yet there is not necessarily any relationship between money spent and personal satisfaction. We buy yachts that go out into the seas a few times then forever stay put in a slip at shore. Purchasing expensive diving gear and going out into the ocean sounded like fun from the ads but we quickly discover that's not really our thing. We spend thousands on exotic vacations to faraway places only to have a miserable time and come back home feeling irritable and worn out. Every New Year's Eve we go to the same noisy places, drink too much and start the new year with a headache and a hangover.

By asking yourself what you really want to do, you will find yourself less at the mercy of fads, commercial interests and others' influence.

Take a look at the people in your life. If you were to list the six people most important to you, who would they be and how much time are you spending with them? It is easy to get ourselves into situations where others who we have little in common with are taking up much of our time.

A neighbor may telephone "just to chat" when you are right in the middle of a project. A casual acquaintance may drop by because she or he has nothing better to do and disrupt your day or evening. At one time or another this happens to all of us. And the minutes and hours can add up.

Finally, in taking stock of our leisure, it is important to consider not only what we are doing but our motivation. We may participate in different activities for any number of reasons, and derive various benefits from them. One person may jog to insure physical fitness while another may go jogging because he or she is getting pressure from their mate or friends.

We join clubs and organizations out of social concern because we want to see changes come about. We join groups to meet people socially, have friends and make business contacts. We may travel out of curiosity or as an escape from boredom. Playing the stock market may be a fun hobby, a serious endeavor for financial gain or both.

Think about the pastimes and social activities you are

involved in. What portion of your time is spent on activities for physical fitness? For creativity? Personal growth and learning? Financial rewards? What kinds of activities do you find relaxing? And how much time is spent out of boredom, obligation and due to demands and pressures from others?

There is no one pattern of activities that is right or wrong. Each of us has a different set of needs, values and expectations. The question to ask yourself is only, what's right for you? By taking time to become more aware of how your discretionary time is spent and pinpointing areas of satisfaction and dissatisfaction you then have the power to bring about change.

*Greater Success and Prosperity Through Leisure*

In past history only a small privileged and elite class had much leisure, mostly as a function of slave labor. Today with modern medical advances, flexitime, longer vacations and the shorter workweek, each person has the PROMISE of more leisure and a more rewarding life style. Dare to take time. Then do what YOU really find interesting, valuable or challenging.

It is easy to get swallowed up in tasks and activities to the extent that we find ourselves responding more than deciding. In order to have time for the many things we want to do, we need to carve out that spare time for ourselves.

Leisure and success are a two-way street and go hand in hand. With greater success we can have increased leisure, and with more leisure, our opportunities for success and prosperity are virtually unlimited.

Leisure power means taking control to create the kinds of successes you desire, whether they be personal, social or financial. In the face of today's volatile economy, achieving financial success solely through a job is highly improbable. We can no longer work at our job and confidently tuck our earnings away in blue chip stocks or bonds and expect to come out ahead (if ever we could). Only by setting aside some of our spare time to educate ourselves as wiser consumers and investors are we likely to stretch out our dollars, conquer inflation and achieve financial prosperity.

Leisure power means making the kinds of choices that will result in FREEDOM FROM those things in our lives that are holding us back and preventing us from achieving prosperity. These may be internal constraints such as procrastination, self-doubts or apathy as well as those forces in our environment that act to shape and seduce us into doing a lot of things we do not wish to do, enjoy doing or find beneficial.

Leisure power also means FREEDOM TO recognize and pursue the many opportunities that are available to us.

*Explore Your Hopes and Dreams...Then Act*

Happiness is a by-product of progressing toward our hopes and dreams. Determine what you want by brainstorming. Take a sheet of paper and list all the things you would like to do, have or be. It may be going hang gliding off Makapu, having a loving relationship, or being 15 pounds lighter. Let yourself go and free associate.

For the time being, forget about how unrealistic your dreams might sound. Let me share with you a personal experience that I believe you will find helpful. Growing up in the Midwest, one of my fondest dreams was to live on a tropical island surrounded by ocean. I also wanted to continue my research in personality, creativity and leisure, and to have a career whereby I could contribute to others understanding here. Shortly after graduating from the University of Illinois, I decided to act on this dream. Without a whole lot of thought, but a strong belief that I was doing the right thing, I packed my bags and moved to the island of Oahu, Hawaii.

Upon arriving I checked in at Moana Lua Residence Halls on the University of Hawaii campus, and with high hopes and my usual enthusiasm for new ventures began my job search. I didn't know anyone on the island but was soon to meet a number of kamaainas (Hawaiian locals). With the best of intentions they told me - friendly but firmly - that my best bet was to leave immediately and go back to Mainland, U.S.A. The universities and colleges were definitely NOT hiring; Ph.D.'s were roaming the streets or sweeping the streets. "DIDN'T I KNOW that Honolulu was one of the most competitive job markets around? At best I would be able to land a job as a dishwasher in a Waikiki hotel, as a taxi driver or as a cocktail waitress."

I don't mean to disparage any of these occupations but that just was not what I had in mind. I had spent enough time in the kitchen; dishes could best be done by a machine. My love of driving is something less than my joy for fighting crowds at Christmas time. And coming to live in one of the healthiest climates in the world to spend my time inside a smoke-filled cocktail lounge as a waitress was out of the question.

In spite of the pronouncements of the kamaainas, within a few months I found myself in front of a class of eager students at the university. I continued to teach and do research for the five years I was in Hawaii before coming to San Francisco and founding Uptime.

Capturing my dream and turning it into a reality used basically the same approach as the contest hobby. I did everything I could to increase my odds. Before going on an interview (and I went on a lot), I researched the college or university and the department to which I was applying. I wrote down what I felt I could contribute and followed up with a letter, phone call or in person. As far as I was concerned neither the competition nor anything else had any bearing on my fate: it was up to me. I honestly BELIEVED that I would be successful in what I wanted to do.

You too will be as successful as you decide to be.

After you have listed your dreams and wishes, go through them again and ask yourself what you really want and why. If you do not have a strong motivation, the first time something comes along to interfere with your aspirations, you will falter. As a measure of your desire you might ask yourself what you would be willing to give up in order to obtain it. Recognize the sacrifices that may go along with your decisions and deal with them mentally BEFORE you act.

Important decisions are never easy and a certain amount of risk (whether it be psychological, physical or financial) is always imminent. But if you assess the risk and deal with it before you act, you will not later be burdened with guilt and self-doubts about having made the wrong decision.

## Making a Commitment to Leisure

"Leisure offers a marvelous opportunity for freedom to be exercised, but where there is no commitment that freedom becomes aimlessness or apathy." (Robert Lee)

Too often what happens in our leisure is incidental to our lives. In our work, we set goals, establish priorities and make deadlines. Yet in our personal lives, everything is frequently up for grabs.

Much of our orientation from early childhood, throughout high school and college has been toward the planning and preparation for a career. For decades we have been concerned about finding meaning, self-fulfillment and receiving financial gain through our work. However, even in the best of jobs, these expectations cannot always be met.

One of my clients who heads a large corporation once told me that he found his work stimulating and challenging, yet in keeping a Time Reactor Log and recording his reactions to daily tasks, he discovered that less than 15 % of his duties were challenging or provided any opportunities for creativity. Another client who is a dedicated teacher estimated that with test taking time, grading papers, keeping discipline and meetings, no more than 20 % of her time was meaningful in terms of communicating ideas, stimulating curiosity and interest in the classroom.

HOW MUCH MORE POTENTIAL WE HAVE FOR STIMULATION, CREATIVITY AND PERSONAL DEVELOPMENT IN OUR LEISURE HOURS. In the course of history many of our finest achievements in the arts, sciences and humanities have been made by persons outside of the work setting and during leisure time. Leonardo da Vinci and Benjamin Franklin are well known examples of men who achieved much outside of their everyday work. Chaucer, one of the world's greatest poets, earned his living as a collector of customs. Mendel was the abbot of a monastary but managed to make major breakthroughs in genetics during his free hours. Some of our most gifted novelists have been practicing physicians.

One of the key elements in these achievements was a sense of freedom and playfulness. Being able to play around with ideas, words or symbols and being free from pressures and time constraints can open the door to innovations and creativity.

Another factor was a sense of purpose and commitment in their leisure...taking a block of time and shaping it into a work of art, a dream, a vision, a tangible creation.

You may not aspire to be the world's greatest poet or a

science wizard, but it is during your leisure hours - that time when you are freest to be yourself - that you can realize the best from yourself and truly experience leisure power.

*"All that we are is the result of what we have thought."*
*Buddha*

*"I am fully convinced that the soul is indestructible, and that its activity will continue through eternity. It is like the sun, which, to our eyes, seems to set in night; but it has in reality only gone to diffuse its lights elsewhere."*
Goethe

The Enlightenment Amplifiers

**DICK CALDWELL**
38-1011 Canterbury Dr. S.W.
Calgary, Alberta, Canada T2W 2Si
(403) 281-2040   238-0803

## DICK CALDWELL

Dick Caldwell has been appearing before audiences, in one form or another, for over twenty years. As a nightclub entertainer, singer, M.C., comedian and platform speaker, he has presented programs in 40 states, eight provinces and all through Southeast Asia, including a performance before the King and Queen of Thailand. He has also worked on a chicken farm, a hat factory, as a private secretary, a claims agent for a trucking company, salesman, sales manager and booking agent.

Born, reared and educated in Pennsylvania, he has lived in Florida, Michigan, Louisiana, West Virginia, Washington, Virginia and Oregon. He currently makes his home in Calgary, Alberta, Canada with his wife and two teen-age children.

Dick's professional speaking career began shortly after he won the 1979 World Speaking Competition of Toastmasters International. His message is: You do have the power to succeed! There is nothing wrong with having a dream! You can turn your dream into reality! Dick believes that with all his heart and welcomes the opportunity to pass his discoveries on to others. As he says, "This has worked for me - it can work for you."

# THE POWER OF A DREAM

*By Dick Caldwell*

*"I believe.....because we have great dreams and because we have the opportunity to make those dreams come true."*

*Wendell Willkie - Taken from his creed, inscirbed on a marker by his grave in Rushville, Indiana.*

The little gold pin with the number 12 on it is now displayed on a board in my office along with other mementos and awards. I keep it as a reminder of my mother's conscientious effort to provide me with a proper spiritual, as well as educational environment. As a child, I took it for granted that each and every Sunday I would go to Sunday School. The gold pin verifies that for twelve years I did so without missing a week. During that period of time I also took for granted the things that were taught. Looking back, it now appears I took them for granted but perhaps didn't really understand. Perhaps, as a child, I could not understand the subtleties and implications of those teachings; otherwise, how could I find myself, in my mid-twenties, so confused, depressed and lost. My main feelings, at that time in my life, were fear, failure and frustration.

After losing my job, my savings and my family in Florida, I had driven my old Hudson to Charleston, West Virginia to accept a job offer from a friend; a job in direct sales on straight commission, both new to me. I sold what I could, raising just enough money for gas for the trip, knowing I'd have to drive during the cool of the night and stop often because of a faulty radiator which I couldn't afford to have repaired. A friend provided me with a large bag of ham sandwiches and I was on my way.

As I approached Nahunta, Georgia, I was stopped by a local policeman in a three year old Oldsmobile and dressed in civilian clothes except for a cap, badge and gun. Although my car could barely run, he said I was speeding and the fine was to be paid immediately or I'd be put in jail to await a hearing, "in a few days." There went most of my money and by the time I reached South Carolina I had no money for gas. After three unsuccessful attempts to get service station owners to take a check (for which, of course, there were no funds), I pulled into a station, told the attendant to "fill her up", and, as he was removing the hose from my full tank, I got out my check book, started writing and said, "How do you want me to make this out?" "We don't take checks", he said. "I don't know why not", I replied, "all the other stations have." After explaining that I had no cash and it was either accept the check or somehow remove the gas from my car, he begrudingly took the check and off I drove. By repeating this act four or five times, I made it to Charleston to start a new life, and a new job, but full of negative thoughts.

*Becoming a Promise Keeper*

With the help of my friend, Bob Spicher, who gave me

my job as a salesman, I managed to make a living and in two months was able to send money to cover the worthless checks I had written during my journey. Two of the service station owners wrote back expressing their surprise and pleasure at receiving money they had written off as a loss. Although I had an income, my mental condition had not changed much. I wish I could say that I corrected that situation on my own but such was not the case. I now believe we all need someone to guide us in times like that; someone who cares and who can be more objective about our lives than we can, under those kinds of conditions. We need someone who can lead us from the darkness of our own negative thinking and show us the light of our potential; someone who can enlighten us. Fortunately, I found two such people. One became my mentor and friend. The other, whom I met a few months later, was to become my wife.

My territory became Parkersburg, West Virginia, and the surrounding area. One day I called on a prospect in Marietta, Ohio. She was an attractive and intelligent young lady. I was attracted not only to her but to her family. They made me feel welcome and invited me back. I enjoyed seeing her and was fascinated by her father who, although considerably older than myself, became my close friend. He is a salesman, a clinical hypnotist and a teacher; the kind who would answer most of my questions with either a question, a quotation or by giving me a book, saying, "Read this, and we'll discuss it again." One day his daughter said to me, "I have a feeling you're coming here more to see my father than to see me. I think it's time to change your status from boy friend to friend of the family." Now, twenty years later, I still maintain that position and although separated by many miles, when we do see each other, it's as though we're continuing a conversation and relationship interrupted by days instead of months, or years.

*Discover - Learn - Use*

Floyd McGuire started me thinking, questioning and discovering many things. He started me on three stages of development that I feel are necessary for enlightenment. First - Introduction. He introduced to me, through conversation and books, ideas, concepts and knowledge that enabled me to see that first ray of light. Secondly - Assimilation. He showed me the importance of taking advantage of what is available for personal growth, such as books, tapes, listening to others, discussions and organizations. I became aware of the need to not only be exposed to these things, such as I was to Sunday School in my youth, but to digest them, consider them and absorb them for my own use and enlightenment. And thirdly - Utilization. This is the active part; putting into use what you have learned. To benefit from our new-found knowledge, we must give it a chance to work, to prove to ourselves that it can work and will work. These three things led me to the truth: Discover it, learn it and use it.

Without being conscious of what was happening, I became enlightened. I became aware of the unlimited good, prosperity and success available to us all. Prior to that I had heard about positive thinking. I had attended sales meetings where they talked about Positive Mental Attitude. I listened to speakers talk about how we could better use our time, and I'd say what a terrific presentation it was, and them head to a restaurant for a cup of coffee instead of going to work. I had been exposed to all of this but, like the Sunday School lessons of my childhood, I didn't apply these things to myself. Now, there it was. Not a sudden flash, not like a religious conversion or a cosmic illumination, but developing slowly until my change was noticed by others and mentioned to me. It was then I realized that I could control my success and my life, as can anyone else control theirs.

My enlightenment started me on the road to becoming a Positive Power Person. It enabled me to admit that I had dreams and that these dreams could be realized, that I had the power to turn my dreams into reality. Now I could stand up and say, "I have a dream." These four words have undoubtedly been spoken by countless numbers of people, in every language and in every age since the beginning of time. They have probably been spoken, perhaps silently if not out loud, by you. We all remember one of the great leaders in the struggle for human rights who stood in front of the Lincoln Memorial in Washington, D.C. and said, "I have a dream." Martin Luther King stood in front of a monument named after a man who 100 years earlier, in a speech to the Congress of the United States, said "I have a dream." Both of these great men, and others, believed so strongly in their dream they were willing to die for it - and did.

*Power Dreams*

What do you suppose is meant by the phrase, "I have a dream"? I suggest that the dream in the minds of people like Dr. Martin Luther King and Abraham Lincoln and John Kennedy and Golda Meir and Sir John A. McDonald and Henry Ford and John Diefenbaker was that they had a goal, a purpose not only worth dying for but worth working at - something so important that it consumed their mental and physical energy - something so vital to them that it gave them their very reason for living.

Did these people have their dreams, their goals, because they were great? Or do we think of them as great because they had a dream, and dedicated themselves to making it come true?

We all have dreams. Why do some people's dream come true while others look back years later and wonder what might have been if...

In studying the lives of famous people who were successful, and observing the lives of successful people not so famous, I find that one thing they all have in common is this: They all get back up when they're knocked down. As an example - A young man runs for the state legislature and is badly beaten. He next enters business, it fails, and he spends 17 years of his life paying off the debts of a worthless partner. He falls in love with a beautiful young woman to whom he becomes engaged, then she dies. He enters politics, runs for congress and is badly defeated. He tries to get an appointment to the U.S. Land Office and is turned down. He becomes a candidate for the Senate, is defeated, runs again and loses! There's a song that says, "Pick yourself up, dust yourself off, start all over again." That's what Abraham Lincoln did and he is now remembered for what he did after all those setbacks.

I've seen this same spirit at work in my own family. Some years ago my career dictated that I spend a lot of time away from home, often for weeks at a time. As a parent, in a situation like that, you miss a lot. It was especially difficult for me one fall because my son, Victor, was playing on a Pee Wee football team that hadn't lost a game that season, and I hadn't been home to see a game all season. Vic told me on the phone it was his dream to play in the city championship and have me there to see the game. By the end of the regular season, Vic's team was undefeated and scheduled against the defending champions in the city play-offs. I caught a plane the morning of the game and arrived at the stadium just before kick-off. The whistle blew and for four quarters I watched our team play their hearts out and still suffer such a beating it wasn't even a contest. When the gun went off ending the game, it was a very depressed group of eleven-year-olds that left the field. I walked down to the edge of the field and as my son approached me, fighting back the tears, he looked up and said, "Well, you're here - and I never said it was my dream to win the championship." And then as he walked away, he added, "But you just wait until next year."

Time and time again we hear stories like these. Everyone, in and out of the entertainment industry, thought Frank Sinatra was washed up until he managed to get a part in the motion picture "From Here to Eternity", which started him back on the road of success that has continued for so many years.

Many people thought Sammy Davis's career had come to an end when a tragic automobile accident left him with only one eye. The late actor, Jeff Chandler, then at the height of his own career, reinforced Sammy's already strong faith by offering one of his own eyes. Wearing first a patch, and then a glass eye, Sammy Davis continued performing and has become a legend in his own time.

Is it not obvious that it was the dream in the hearts and minds of these people that kept them going when many would have given up? A dream, seen in the mind and felt in the heart that was too big to be denied.

## The First Step

We all have dreams. But how do you turn dreams into reality? First, you must transfer your dream into a goal, and your goal into a plan. Volumes have been written about setting and achieving goals. The very fact that you are reading this book indicates that you are the kind of person who is interested in improving your life and your situation. Being that kind of person, you probably have read something relating to goal setting. But don't you think the very fact that there is so much written on the subject points to the importance of it? No winning coach would send his team on the field without a game plan. No experienced sea captain would set sail without first having carefully charted his course. No salesperson becomes a top producer without first planning his work and then working his plan.

## The Second Step

The second step in turning your dream into a reality is to picture yourself as having already reached your goal. Earl Nightengale lectures that we become what we think about and I agree with Mr. Nightengale that by thinking as many times during the day as we can about the goal we've established for ourselves, we actually begin moving toward it, and bringing it toward us. In order to do this we must believe that what we envision for ourselves will come to pass, that it's already happening, that a Universal Law decrees that it cannot be otherwise. You must appreciate the fact that your desires, ideas, dreams, are all real in your mind, though invisible. To know that your idea is real, that it has form, shape, and substance on the mental plane, and that it is as real as your hand on the objective plane, gives you scientific faith and enables you to have a conviction deep in your subconscious mind. It has been said, "What the mind of man can conceive, and believe, it can achieve."

During the period of time that I worked as a nightclub entertainer, I had a very talented dancer work for me. Although she was gifted and had spent years training and practicing, she was sure she would never really get anywhere because of her height. You see, this girl is 5'4" tall and most shows and acts want dancers who are tall and leggy. She confided in me that her dream was to work in a show in Las Vegas but that she was just about ready to give up. She had done quite a few auditons, was always complimented on her ability, but always told they were looking for a "different type." When I disbanded my act to pursue other interests, I told her to go to Las Vegas, keep practicing, continue going to auditions, and constantly maintain a picture in her mind of dancing in a show at one of the big hotels. Borrowing an idea from Maxwell Maltz, I told her to act and think like a lead dancer would act and think, and to have faith. She became enthused enough to give it a try. Although she took a few out-of-town jobs to pay the bills, as I write this chapter, she is the featured dancer in a revue at a hotel on the Las Vegas "strip" where the lead singer is 5'8" and needed comparatively short dancers to compliment him.

*The Third Step*

The third thing necessary to realize your dream is that ingredient that separates a person with a dream from a person who is just a dreamer - work. My Pennsylvania Dutch mother once gave me a plaque that reads, "All things cometh to he who waiteth; if he worketh like a son-of-a-gun while he waiteth." I sometimes think too many people remember the part of the book that says, "as you believe, so shall it be", but forget the part that says, "as you sow, so shall you reap." There is nothing wrong with having a dream, no matter how farfetched it might seem to others. It doesn't matter what others think. Whoever thought someone would get rich selling pet rocks? Hang on to your dream. Keep it secret or share it with your loved ones, whichever suits you. But, while you're dreaming, go out and do something to bring it closer to coming true. The man who made a fortune telling others how to succeed, Earl Nightengale, put it this way: Have a purpose in life, and having it, throw such strength of mind and muscle into your work as God has given you.

So, dream your dream. Have a plan, think positive, work hard, and believe! This has worked for me, it can work for you. By following these ingredients, I was able to quit my job as a salesman (although I later went back to sales for awhile, but by my own choice), and go back to my first love, entertaining. Using the concepts just mentioned I overcame the obstacles of re-starting with very little money, less "natural" talent than many, no effective connections in the music business, no agent, no long-term contracts and a new family to support. By believing in my dream, and with the support of my wife, I put together a show that ultimately played in 40 states, eight provinces of Canada, and all through Southeast Asia, highlighted by a performance for the King and Queen of Thailand. When I retired from that profession, it was by choice to pursue a new career, at age 43, in public speaking in order to share my discoveries with others.

We live in an age where there is more help available than ever before to guide you towards your own enlightenment. We live in one of the few countries in the world where our rewards are still in direct proportion to our efforts. If you will take advantage of those two facts, you too can stand confident and secure when you say, "I have a dream!"

The Enlightenment Amplifiers

CATHERINE E. WIANDS, R.M.H.
Changing Attitudes (Home of "Transitions")
7730 Herschel Avenue, Suite J
La Jolla, California 92037
(714) 454-8471    (714) 566-2326

## CATHERINE WIANDS

Catherine Wiands, Registered Master Hypnotist and motivational counselor, completed her hypnosis training in 1977 and became one of only 9,000 Master Hypnotists in the United States (very few females). She then went into intensive self-study developing her own seminar, "TRANSITIONS". Transitions, a "Fix-it-yourself" seminar demonstrates how to live your life by direction and not by accident, using hypnosis as a tool for eliminating negative restrictive behavior patterns and replacing them with positive modes.

Working coast to coast with a variety of organizations, Catherine's ability to captivate an audience is known and appreciated. She enjoys tailoring each "Transitions" workshop to meet the needs of those in attendance. Clients learn, among other things, to develop confidence, memory, concentration, special skills and the ability to relax. They also learn how to eliminate such things as procrastination, overweight, smoking, and fear of success. Catherine is especially effective in showing how to use self hypnosis as a practical tool for better personal and interpersonal communication. She extends this technique to affect better time management and organizational effectiveness.

Ms. Wiands is the founder and director of Changing Attitudes in La Jolla, CA., where she uses her skill as Master Hypnotist working with individuals. She has produced a number of recordings, each one designed to effect a specific change in an individual's life.

Catherine is available to entertain and inform groups across the United States. She also is a member of the Hypnotists Examining Council, Hypnotists Union, World Congress of Hypnotists, Women in Sales and various motivational and civic groups in San Diego.

Catherine is the mother of two teenagers Deborah 18, and Skip 17. She is a new bride and is back in college majoring in psychology.

**18**

POSITIVE
power
PEOPLE

*The Enlightenment Amplifiers*

# YOUR GREATEST
# POWER: MIND

*By Catherine Wiands*

*"He who knows others is wise. He who knows himself is enlightened."*
*Unknown, from Familiar Quotations*

*"The Light Dawned*

I salt bolt upright in bed!...Something had happened! I didn't know exactly what it was, but something had hit me...I had been shut away in my bedroom, in apathy and in pain from a back injury sustained in an automobile accident, for over 11 months; only going out when absolutely necessary...I had quit a job I really liked because of the pain, separated from my husband of 14 years, and began to deteriorate. I had sunk into apathy...

But, something happened that day...

As I sat there wide-eyed, all alone, it suddenly occurred to me that if I kept on living this way, I'd be a suicide case, or die of natural causes. I was like they say in the movies. My whole life flashed in front of me. I look back now mentally as I write this and remember asking myself what I was all about? I asked myself what I had contributed to the world.

## *Who Was Catherine Wiands?*

As I reflected, I saw a lady who had held jobs which varied from waitressing part time to jobs carrying a great deal of responsibility; in addition to having my children and raising my children alone; my husband was military and was seldom home. Among other things, I was instrumental in the implementation of American dependent employment in Yokohama, Japan. I half smiled to myself. That was no easy task, but I had accomplished it and did it well. The living conditions for dependents was less than desirable, I knew we had some very talented but very depressed women there and that if they were busy, things would be better. It was a big chunk to chew but as I got involved, I was also asked to maintain all of the paperwork persuant to American employment and I loved it...(I trained these ladies) I had also been a very successful real estate salesperson...until my husband made me quit. I had been the only person in my position with the government to be promoted at that desk, and with a merit achievement award on top of that. I had built a clientelle of over 700 with cosmetics in door to door sales in three months in Fallon, Nevada. As I focused in on all of those things, I suddenly felt a new strength inside of me. It must have been Positive Power that hit me that day. I suddenly knew that I had a lot left to do before I just could lay down and die...I also realized that I had better get reinvolved with life and become more of a mother to my children. They needed me. Okay, I recognized the problem, now what was I going to do about it???

## *Hypnosis, a Key*

I had seen advertisements in the classified section of the newpaper, but I knew nothing about hypnosis, like most people. I purchased a newspaper. I found the most recent ad. It told of an upcoming free lecture. I decided to attend. After all I had just remembered about myself, I couldn't be a quitter now! That was the first step to the beginning of the new me. What I heard that night really sparked something way down deep inside of me.

The speaker told me I could have confidence, regain my excellent memory (that may not mean much to some people, but I was so bad at that time that if I went from the bedroom to get something in the kitchen by the time I'd get there, I'd forget why I was there). She told me I could have success if I wanted it. I could change my life. As Carol Baras spoke I became more and more alive. The hope that had been lost for the last few years of my life suddenly sprang forth. I had switched from the flight to the fight instinct.

My mind was sharp and clear. I was like a sponge absorbing every word. The most astounding bit of information received was that "I" was the cause of my own experiences; that everything follows thought; that we become the sum total of our thinking patterns. Boy, I didn't like coming to grips with that idea, but it all made so much sense. I continued listening. I was born that night! I signed up for the self-hypnosis program and also encouraged an old friend to attend too. You see, we attract what we are on a mental level by way of associations. Joyce Coyne and I were on similiar paths. The amazing thing is, that very lady ultimately became the very reason that I wound up in my chosen profession. Proves the theory, that if you help enough people get what they want, you get everything you want. I took the program and I practiced self-hypnosis religiously. I read every book concerning self improvement and positive thinking I could get my hands on. I studied the theory and proper application of affirmations and utilized everything I learned! I had 76 affirmations which I used every day in my life. Seventy-six things I wanted to change about myself. I still remember driving all over San Diego in 80 degree plus temperatures with no air conditioning, windows up singing "I have more self-confidence than I've ever had before" - it worked!

I went from that basket case; from a hateful, neurotic, hostile, sickly lady to one of the happiest, most contented ladies you'll ever meet...From a recluse, to a national speaker...sure, it has taken five years, but let me share with you some of the things which have transpired along the way...

*Self Awareness*

One of the most exciting phases of my life was getting to know Catherine Wiands...

I took time to organize my life. I began taking time for myself. I read. I read. I read some more. I took notes. I kept a "thought diary". I wrote down many thoughts that "occurred" to me on a daily basis. This enabled me to analyze my thought pattern. I discovered I had a sense of humor. I discovered I was creative after all. Catherine Wiands was changing day by day.

During my professional Hypnosis classes I suddenly had the idea that somehow, someway I'd be involved with hypnosis professionally. I didn't know how. I looked my life over. I realized I must have a way with people and selling ability. I was convinced of the greatest power human beings have, "the power of mind". I prepared for the examination to receive my Master Hypnotist Certification. Where 100 clinical hours were required I earned 300. Where 100 practical application hours were required I worked over 400 hours out of my home with hundreds of people "No Charge". I had to prove to myself hypnosis worked and that I was prepared to dedicate myself to it. As I excelled in this, I developed my own feelings of self worth.

As I got to know myself better, I utilized many of the concepts I now present with conviction in my transitions seminar.

## Finding Priorities

If you take a deck of cards, throw it up into the air and watch the cards fall..can you pick up the entire deck with one swoop of your hand? Not likely..and a friend of mine reminded me of that fact. She watched me becoming more and more frustrated in my attempt to raise my children perfectly...keep an immaculate home, get a business started, and keep my personal life intact. I digested that idea for a few days, then made a decision. The most important of all things was that I have my house and home in order.

I realized that I couldn't leave a house that was all askew and go out and teach. I realized also that I couldn't speak of love, understanding, success, etc. if I didn't practice it in my life. I spent two solid weeks of hard "work" to get my house in order.

I wallpapered in bright colors, painted, did yard work, cleaned closets, spent time with my children, it worked! As each chore was completed, I felt better. Seeing the smiles on my children's faces was beautiful.

## One More Try

As I was making my own "transistion" it became necessary to take one last shot at rebuilding my marriage. I guess in my mind at the time, it was like atoning for all past mistakes. I was ready now to take charge of my life and accept all responsibility for myself, and in doing so I recognized that I had also contributed considerably to the breakdown of the marriage.

My husband had left ahead of the family to a new duty

station, Scotland. We had passport applications to join him in June, he had left in March. To make a long story short, Easter Sunday we received a beautiful card and money for Easter Breakfast, and on my birthday the following week, a dear Jane and kids. My husband had run into a high school sweetheart, just divorced.

I learned the hard way, that you can't go back. It is always exciting to me when I share this message with clients and listeners of my tapes and seminars. It gives me reinforcement too each time I share it. It is so much more beneficial to close the door gently on the past and become a today person, a now person. You block all good from your life when you sink into the past...what happened in the past happened. You can decide to take some course of action which will free you from any guilt, or negative feelings. If you do, O.K. Win, lose or draw. Then, you can go on with your life. It took two broken ribs and very painful emotional struggle to learn this lesson. It set my career back considerably. I fought desperately not to go back into that room though. And I won.

I began dating again after the encounter with my husband. I believe it was enlightenment to recognize that you attract what you are by way of association. If your actions and attitudes are negative and hostile; if you haven't accepted yourself - really, you attract partners in that same frame of mind. With that enfoldment, I stopped dating and went into solitude. Some people look at being alone as being painful; I did earlier. Now I cherish the quiet times, the alone times. I recognize the need for them. When you slow down - that's when Positive Power can really touch your life.

*Children are People Too*

It saddened me so to look at my beautiful children, Deborah 13, and Skip aged 12 and see the confusion and hurt. If I as an adult was having trouble understanding why their father left, they must really be suffering as children. They didn't know why I had shut myself away in that room either. I made the decision to do something for 'us' as a little family of three. Eureka - that's it! Why not take the children to see their grandparents in Nantucket, Mass.? I could include the children in my work, and I could earn our trip. I had driven across country alone with the children in the past so driving would be no problem. I could get to know my children and at the same time give them a pleasant experience to look back on. We all needed it. The children were a perfect age to appreciate this beautiful country too! I became really excited. It wouldn't be long before my children would be raised and away to live their own lives so I better enjoy them all I can while they are still home. It was painful to acknowledge that it was time to begin loosening the apron strings, and allow my childred to grow and develop into adults. Children are people too!

*About Transitions*

I had kept all of the "special interest - to me" items from hundreds of self-help and motivational books I had read in two spiral notebooks. I spotted an ad in the classified section of the paper "hypnotists wanted". I went to, yup, another free lecture. As I listened, I realized I had my own program in progress. Why hadn't I thought of presenting seminars? I came very close to signing up with this company, but one of the considerations was that they wanted me to drop the 'Master' from my title for which I had worked so hard; not counting all of my accident money paying for the special training. I reviewed their instruction manual and in my own mind my information would be more instructional and informative in the area of hypnosis, and effecting positive behavior changes using self-hypnosis as a vehicle.

At that point I made the decision to organize my own program and market it. I researched the market. I wrote many affirmations to sharpen my speaking skills on a professional level. I prepared myself emotionally and physically to present my program. I had to build-in the ability to accept constructive criticism too because I knew there would be some in the beginning. I made darn sure that I knew the material I wanted to present backward and forward. This wasn't all my idea. I had an excellent instructor and he assisted me in the sense that he stated the criteria for being a good speaker. I gave myself some literary license too...built in things like magnetic personality...and the ability to relate to any group in any place at any time. I really used my Positive Power because I also slipped in an affirmation that my subconscious mind would guide me in all presentations in a way that my material would be interesting to that group where I was. I could go on about this forever...it proved to be very successful.

First and foremost was the education of what hypnosis was all about and how to utilize it to develop potential...or to just relax, or...I had a great deal of information to share and clarity in how I wanted to present it. It was and is very important to me to give hypnosis validity as a powerful and effective method of developing potential...I wanted to remove the mystery and doubt surrounding hypnosis. Everything really just fell into place. I'd been putting the program together, really for over 3 years. I outlined and "structured" Transition. All of this, by the way, was the manifestation of an affirmation I made two years previously and kind of forgot. The beauty of it all is I was on automatic in a beam of Positive Power and didn't even realize how strong the light was. I had that compulsion to write, write and write not knowing why. All of my affirmations were manifesting!

I made the decision to have a "fix-it-yourself" type program. People cannot change unless they make the decision themselves and do the work themselves. You can only change yourself. I went back to where I learned self-hypnosis and repeated the program. One more decision was made. I would have a spontaneous workshop style program. The size of the group would remain small and each attendee would receive specific information which they could apply to their lives. Transitions is like my hair...the color changes, the length changes, the style changes but the foundation is strong and the basics remain the same.

Once again, I decided to play it safe and present my first seminar in a comfort zone - military bases. After all, I'd been a military wife so long, I knew if I made a mistake, I'd be forgiven more easily. I was one of them! It worked well. I presented several of my then unnamed seminars. I think one of the things that made me do this so successfully was that my husband had said I'd never pull it off.

After I proved I could work this out and worked at all of the local bases, and also Mass. I decided that staying around the military uniforms was too painful. This way of life for me after many years was too painful. I began setting a seminar up on what is termed by the military as the outside. Once again, I covered myself. I scheduled the first big civilian program over an entire weekend, two classes each day, one a.m. and one p.m., on what would have been my fifteenth wedding anniversary. What a wise thing this was! I had over forty people, drawn from a "free" lecture I did. Could it be I caught on to a perfect technique? It was exciting! It was profitable! I "forgot" so easily what day it was! I had earned enough money too to take my children to Nantucket ALL EXPENSES PAID!

*Frosting On The Cake*

I bolstered the courage to set up a seminar on Nantucket as well, and it was fantastic. There has been a lot of growth since then. I opened the doors to my new

business 'Changing Attitudes" in La Jolla, CA. in May of
1977. The growth of the business where I do individual
consultations and work with small groups and "Transitions" has been incredible. From one relaxation tape
with a hand written label to a full catalog of tapes
packaged beautifully, distributors nationally and sales
internationally in less than 2 years. Oh, by the way, in my
spare time I remarried.

My new husband, James Annett has been a true
support system. He inspires, coaches and encourages me
in everything in a most loving way. By providing an even
balance in the home he makes it possible for me to grow
professionally. This man also writes in the most
descriptive and imaginative way. I often relate material
he has written to my classes. Just watching the
responses I know James is headed for greatness. I could
very easily be a workaholic because I love my work so, but
he also generates "creative escapes", needed by both of
us.

From a basket case to a very happy person, a person
with a feeling of self-worth, in five short years...You can
change your life too! All you have to do is decide what it is
you want to change. It is your right, your privilege and
your obligation to yourself to live a happy and rewarding
life...Positive Mental Control is the most important
behavior to develop. Become a Positive Power Person by
learning more about the power of mind.

In conclusion, I no longer question:

* What the force was behind the man who had seen me
crying on the steps of the federal building, stopped and
asked me what was wrong.

* What the force was which compelled me to tell him, a
total stranger what WAS wrong.

* What the force was which caused him to open his very
old briefcase take out an original hardbound copy of
"THINK AND GROW RICH", autograph it and give it
to me.

* What the force was which had me reading that, and

every other book I could intensively, for over 2 1/2 years, and writing, not knowing why, and later discovering I'd written a seminar.

* What made my office available suddenly, in an area I'd mentally chosen.

* What guided me to hypnosis and speaking...To the "Transitions" way of life.

I KNOW NOW...IT WAS POSITIVE POWER!!!

*"Increase of power begets increase of wealth."*
*Cowper*

*"Responsibilities gravitate to the person who can shoulder them. Power flows to the one who knows how."*
*Elbert Hubbard*

POSITIVE POWER PEOPLE

The Enlightenment Amplifiers

**BEVEALY NADLLER**
150-10 79th Avenue
Flushing, New York 11367
(212) 591-4167

## BEVEALY NADLLER

*You've come a long way, baby!* That famous slogan describes Bevealy Nadller perfectly. From a shy, insecure girl, she has become a dynamic professional woman who lectures to thousands of people, and motivates them to literally change their lives.

Bevealy adds a new dimension to professional speaking with her exciting lectures and seminars on Holistic Health. She covers such important subjects as: the New Nutrition, Your Subconscious Mind, Motivation, Better Communication, Stress Reduction, Holistic Approach to Permanent Weight Loss and others.

In addition to lecturing, Bevealy is in private practice as a nutrition consultant and holistic health counselor. She is a frequent guest on talk shows around the country, and writes articles for professional and news publications.

She has studied with some of the most eminent health researchers, and appears on lecture platforms with such noted personalities as Dr. Hans Selye, Dr. E. Cheraskin, Dr. Norman Vincent Peale and Dr. Robert Schuller. Her many professional memberships include: National Speakers Association, International Health Institute, and New York Academy of Sciences.

Bevealy's biographic sketch appears in Who's Who in American Women and Who's Who in American Jewry. She has received many awards and commendations.

Along with her career she enjoys her personal life with husband Phill, a chiropractor, and three teenage daughters.

Ask Bevealy how she manages it all and she takes no credit. "Release that Power within you" she tells you, "and there's no telling what you can accomplish!"

**1 9**

POSITIVE

**POWER**

**PEOPLE**

*The Enlightenment Amplifiers*

# DISCOVER THE DYNAMIC POWER IN YOU

*By Bevealy Nadller*

*"Imagination is the beginning of creation. You imagine what you desire; you will what you imagine; and at last you create what you will."*

*George Bernard Shaw*

The most important event in my life was the discovery that there is an incredible Power within me and that when I tune into it, my life is filled with more health, wealth, success, and happiness.

This Power is all knowing, all seeing, in everything and all powerful. It is Creative Energy of the universe - the Power that man called God.

Oh yes, I believed in God - a mysterious, stern, somewhat forboding figure up in the sky somewhere - distant, unreachable, impersonal. He decided what happened to people - who would be lucky, and would never quite "make it". I was certain I belonged to the second group - until that special day!

*Thoughts are Things*

I remember it well. I had just finished reading "THE DYNAMIC LAWS OF PROSPERITY" by Catherine Ponder. My mind was spinning. This woman, a Unity Minister, was saying that thoughts are things; our thoughts mean something - that with our thoughts we determine and shape our lives - that they serve as a "direct line" to God. Furthermore, she said that God always answers us. He gives us what we believe in, what we expect, what we think about - not necessarily what we want.

What did I believe in? I asked myself. I believed in failure - or at least in "not quite succeeding". I believed in confusion, in fear, in mediocrity. I had never really been successful in anything I had attempted. I was married with three children but I was not content. My life was in a state of confusion. I had many fears - fear of insecurity, fear of accidents, fear of responsibility. I had to admit I lived a mediocre, unfilled life.

I would like to be able to tell you that as soon as I read this book I became a successful, happy, fearless, harmonious person. But it wasn't quite that simple.

My life did change because I realized that the Power to direct my life was inside of me - that I was responsible for me. Knowing that my thoughts, attitudes and beliefs determine, to a large degree, what I experience, I became aware of what I was thinking, feeling and saying. I knew that when I tune into this Power I tap my own Creative Mind. New ideas, inspirations, new ways of looking at things, better ways of relating to others come to me - almost as if an invisible voice is speaking. There is a storehouse of knowledge in everyone's subconscious mind and by tapping this Power we have access to it.

*The Power of Affirmations*

In the DYNAMIC LAWS OF PROSPERITY there

were many positive affirmations - statements to repeat to ourselves in order to change beliefs in our subconscious mind. Affirmations can be short and simple such as: 'I, Bevealy Nadller, am successful, happy and healthy!'', or they can be long and detailed. I wrote my first affirmation that day and I continue to say affirmations each day and night. I have also trained my children to say them.

Affirmations are extremely powerful. In the Bible it says: "and the Word was God". Speak the words with emphasis and authority and use your name. It might interest you to know that in Hebrew the word for God, Soul and "I am" are the same. When you say "I am", you are literally talking to God. Make sure that whatever you say about yourself is positive. Say things like "I am intelligent", "I am happy", "I am healthy", "I am strong".

*The Power of Creative Visualization*

It was in this book that I was introduced to Creative Visualization. "What in the world was creative visualization?" I wondered. The author told me to close my eyes and use my imagination to visualize things the way I want them to be, instead of the way they actually are. This procedure was supposed to help change my life. "Ridiculous," I thought. It sounded like magic and I didn't believe in magic.

Then I got caught up in the idea and I wanted to believe it, so I decided to try. But what should I visualize? I wanted to see immediate results; therefore I needed to visualize something that could happen the following day. I would visualize my three children smiling. You see, every morning my three girls came into my bedroom whining and complaining. When I'd wake up they would always be there-unhappy. Naturally, this started my day off on the wrong side. That evening I spent 15 minutes visualizing my daughters, ages 2, 4, and 7, in my bedroom with big, bright smiles on their faces. I "saw" the bedroom and I saw myself asleep and imagined the girls in their Dr. Denton's climbing out of their beds - wide-eyed and happy - coming into our bedroom. I went to sleep with that wonderful picture filling my mind. The next day I learned to believe in miracles! For there they were smiling at me; one of them even had a flower in her hand that she had made for me. I hugged them all excitedly and declared: "This is a wonderful day - the beginning of many wonderful days!"

### The Power in Negative Situations

And it was! It was also the beginning of many trials and much pain, for I had made a vow - that the most important thing in my life was to grow as a person and to understand the Power within me to the best of my ability. When a negative person makes that decision, there is a difficult road ahead, for in the process of growth there are so many lessons to be learned. Unfortunately, we usually learn our lessons through adversity.

Look back on your life. Has it been a bed of roses? Of course not. Reflect on some of the difficult times. What did you learn from them when the experience was over? If you learned nothing from them, you have a wonderful opportunity to go back over them mentally and see how you could have used the situation for your own self-growth. During difficulties we can throw up our hands in despair, or use the situation to evolve. When we do the latter, we release our creative potential and gain more Power.

### The Powerful Law of Attraction

By the law of attraction each one of us draws to our life those people, conditions, and circumstances that are in harmony with our own thoughts and feelings. What we project comes back to us. Therefore, regardless of the events that are going on around you, use your imagination to visualize things turning out as you'd like them to, not as you fear they will. You will attract more "good fortune" into your life if you focus your attention on the positive aspects. No doubt you've had plenty of experience visualizing the worst; now visualize the best.

If your basic attitudes and belief systems are negative, you will have to work on changing them because they don't change by themselves. Do you know what your attitudes are? When you wake up in the morning what are your thoughts? Is it: "Another good day, God" or "Good God, another day?" Is your cup of life half full or half empty? How you look at things makes all the difference in the world - or at least all the difference in your world.

*Releasing the Power*

Shortly after reading this book I studied Concept-Therapy. It not only confirmed the value of affirmations and creative visualization (also known as mental imagery) but gave me a greater understanding of the magnificence of this Power within us, within all life. I began to see it in everything, in animals, in trees, in all the people that I met. I realized how marvelous it was! I knew that as I tuned into it, I would enjoy life more abundantly on all levels - mental, physical, and spiritual. I learned to set goals, concentrate on them, take suitable action steps and expect to succeed. This was the key to releasing my own creative energy.

I was so thrilled with my new knowledge that I wanted to teach Concept-Therapy. However, first I needed to be able to tell others what I had accomplished using the principles that Concept-Therapy teaches. I had to set a definite goal. I decided to become a singer. I've always loved to sing and I thought I had a pretty good voice. But in the 6th grade a young man that I had a crush on devastated me by saying that I couldn't carry a tune in a basket. I was determined to prove him wrong - eventually.


## The Power of Setting a Goal

When I got married and my husband heard me sing he turned up the radio or shut the door (sometimes he did both). My children suggested that I confine my singing to their bedtime (it put them to sleep). With all this lack of support I began to study singing and I was soon singing semi-professionally. One night at a showcase my husband said the three most important words I could hear at that moment: "You are good!" He was actually talking about my singing! With effort, practice and belief in myself I had accomplished something. But I had not reckoned with the next step in my singing career.

Everytime I had to sing in public strange things happened in my mouth; I got sores on my tongue, pains on my gums, a sore throat, an ache in my tooth, etc. All the symptoms miraculously disappeared after my performance. I observed this with great anxiety and then with understanding. Of course! I was getting these symptoms so that I could not sing. In my subconscious mind I didn't want to sing because of my fears and insecurities, especially in regard to "making a fool of myself". Though I was making progress, by no means had all my negativity disappeared. My creative mind was creating conditions so I couldn't sing. This was a perfect example of how we use our power negatively. However, I knew that if I refused to allow my old beliefs and fears to control me, the symptoms would go away. And they did! In a few months I no longer had any problems in my mouth when I sang (just a queasy feeling in my stomach). Professional singing was now becoming fun!

I never became a star, for there were other goals for me

to fulfill. I had enjoyed my brief career as a singer; I even sang in Rodney Dangerfield's club in New York. But it was time to move on.

## The Power that Motivates

For years - almost from the time I met my husband, a chiropractor, I had been collecting information on natural health. This included information on nutrition, stress, body work, psychological aspects of health and disease, mental imagery, etc. My collection of books, articles, newsletters, clippings, etc. filled the files in my home and my husband's office, and I was running out of room. It seemed as if an unseen force or "Power" was making me explore what would someday become the Holistic Health movement. This led to my attending professional seminars on nutrition and natural health. I was eager to know - and I studied, read, listened, learned. It seemed I had a hunger that could not be satisfied. But I did not know why.

I *did* know that when one is motivated and inclined to carry on an activity with such intensity, there is a reason, and I was sure that someday it would be revealed to me. Meanwhile, I began teaching at the Parker Chiropractic Research Foundation Seminars and spoke to hundreds of chiropractors, their staffs and families. I was teaching some of the most important principles I had learned in Concept-Therapy. But now, I was also counseling my husband's patients on nutrition, and studying psychology; I gradually added these subjects to my lectures at the Parker Chiropractic Research Foundation.

Life seemed to be going along smoothly. My creative mind had inspired many wonderful changes. I thought I really had my "act" together; but I was wrong! An extraordinary experience lay in store for me.

*The Power in Painful Conditions*

One morning in May of 1976 I awakened and could not get out of bed. Walking was sheer agony; in fact it was impossible. The pain was on my left side and extended from my waist to my foot. I assumed I had moved in such a way as to pinch a nerve and that this was causing the excruciating pain. I thought that with rest and a few chiropractic adjustments, I'd be fine. How wrong I was!

I was finally able to walk that day, but only as far as the bathroom. Within the next few days, when I was able to crawl out of bed, I could only walk the equivalent of 1 1/2 blocks before the pain became unbearable. Nevertheless, I was certain that I would be well again. But I did not expect it to take 1 1/2 years!

*The Healing Power*

In the interim I changed my nutritional program, I continued my chiropractic adjustments, I meditated, prayed and practiced mental-imagery. I created an "image" of myself free of pain and saw myself running, jumping and dancing. But nothing changed. Fortunately, I learned about Dr. William Donald Kelley and his Metabolic Nutritional Program. I decided to go on the program and study with Dr. Kelley in Chicago. The program included natural foods, food concentrates and lifestyle changes. I decided to follow the program and "miracle of miracles" in three weeks I was actually walking through Disneyland!

I continued to study with Dr. Kelley and six months later I was certified by the Nutritional Academy (now known as the International Health Institute) as a counselor. My recovery was unusually rapid, no doubt because I had already been doing so many positive things. I needed the final ingredient which the Kelley Program provided; I needed to have my body chemistry balanced so that healing could take place.

I did not get well overnight, but there was a continual improvement from the beginning. In a few months I was free of pain. Now, years later, I realize what a joy it is to walk without the fear of pain. In retrospect, I believe that I needed to experience this condition so I could discover Dr. Kelley's work, and tell others about his program. The Power works in mysterious ways.

By now I was certain that health is the result of many things working harmoniously within the "whole" person - body, mind and spirit. Everything is important - proper nutrition, exercise, rest, body work, positive thoughts and attitudes.

## The Power of Stroking

While recovering from my mysterious ailment I read many personal-development books. One day I passed a bookstore and one book caught my eye. In fact, to my amazement, when I looked in the window it seemed to occupy the entire space. Of course it really didn't occupy the entire window, it just seemed that way. I knew that this was a "signal" and that I was supposed to buy that book. It was "Transactional Analysis in Psychotherapy" by Eric Berne. The book fascinated me. I learned about "stroking", and I realized that in our family we did very little positive stroking.

Originally strokes referred to physical touching, but now the term is used for any form of recognition. Stroking is so important that infants who are not physically handled die of a disease called "miasma", which is actually a shriveling up of their spinal cord. People will do *anything* in order to be stroked. If they are not stroked for their good, positive behavior, they will behave in a negative manner.

It is better to be criticized and stroked unpleasantly than to be ignored. There are many adults who indulge in negative behavior in order to be noticed. This is a carry-over from their youth and it is done outside of their awareness.

## The Power of Communication

In addition to stroking, I learned about ego states. All of us have a "child", "adult", and "parent" ego state. The child part of us is our feeling self. The adult is the thinking, rational self and the parent is the opinionated, critical and nurturing self. For an excellent description of some of the most important aspects of Transactional Analysis and ideas on how you can use it in your own life, I suggest you read I'M OKAY, YOU'RE OKAY by Dr. Thomas Harris and BORN TO WIN by M. James and D. Jongeward. As a result of my TA studies I discovered better ways of communicating with my family. There's a lot of "Power" when family members are in harmony and support each other. By opening channels of communication with people we care about, we actually release our own creative energy.

## The Power of Knowing What You Want

Every new thing I studied added another dimension to my own understanding of health and its many facets. This prepared me for my most ambitious undertaking. Two years ago (in the fall of 1978) I decided to open my own practice as a nutrition consultant and Holistic Health counselor. This would be the culmination of everything I had studied and worked for. I could feel the "Power" in me. All I needed was a suitable space. I searched for one in vain.

After several months a friend asked me: "Bev, what does your office look like?" Frustrated, I replied: "You know I don't have an office yet". "Yes, but what does it look like *in your imagination?*" Of course! I had forgotten the primary rule of goal setting; I had forgotten to visualize my goal. That night I drew a plan of my office. Believe it or not, I found the perfect space the very next day!

The future promises to be most exciting. I am counseling and lecturing to large groups about the concept of Holistic Health - about the importance of harmonizing the body, mind and spirit. I am teaching people how to take care of themselves, and they are enthusiastic and eager to learn - just as I was, and still am. When I speak to a group I can feel the electricity in the room. It is a joy to discover that more and more people are opening their minds and their hearts to free their own creative potential - and discover that dynamic "Power" within!

*"I do not know what I may appear to the world; but to myself I seem to have been only like a boy playing on the seashore, and diverting myself in now and then finding a smoother pebble or a prettier shell than ordinary, while the great ocean of truth lay all undiscovered before me."*
*Sir Isacc Newton*

*"The will to persevere is often the difference between failure and success."*
> David Sarnoff

The Enlightenment Amplifiers

**JOHN M. CROXALL**
John M. Croxall and Associates
1690 Tiburon Blvd.
Tiburon, California 94920
(415) 435-0911    (435) 383-2387

## JOHN CROXALL

John is a successful Financial Planner who has spent thirty years in the financial field, twenty-five of which have been in management.

He is a graduate of Purdue University with a degree in Mechanical Engineering, which gives him an analytical approach to life.

After spending six years in sales he entered the investment industry in 1964 joining Westamerica Securities, Inc., the largest independent broker-dealer specializing in mutual funds in the United States. As Regional Vice President, he developed, from scratch, a California sales organization of fifteen divisions and 150 salespeople whose sales volume in its fourth year was $26 million in mutual fund cash sales, leading all other regions in the 24-year old firm. In 1969 he was featured in an article in Business Week.

In 1974 he decided to devote his energies to teaching personal money management and private practice in counselling people. During the past six years he has personally interviewed and counselled over 2,500 people and has successfully invested over $15 million of their money.

He is past president of the North Bay Chapter of the International Association of Financial Planners and of his local Rotary Club; and is on the teaching staff of both Dominican College and the College of Marin in California.

He has been speaking professionally at meetings and conventions for many years to a wide variety of groups.

# How I Picked Up The Phone And Then Picked Up The Pieces!

*By John Croxall*

*"If you wish success in life, make perseverance your bosom friend, experience your wise counselor, caution your elder brother and hope your guardian genius."*
 *Addison*

It was the summer of 1975 and things had never looked blacker to me. After twenty-one years of marriage, my wife and I had split up. I felt totally responsible and that it was all my fault. So, I signed over to her essentially everything that we had - our home, everything. Everything except a few pieces of office furniture, my car and a $50,000 loan, which I assumed. Here I was in my middle years, $50,000 in debt, and emotionally distraught.

Just before this happened I had decided to start a new career entirely, building my own private practice through conducting financial planning seminars for the public and teaching in the adult education program in Marin County where we lived. Starting any career after twenty-five years in another field is challenging enough in itself with no immediate monetary rewards.

This is the period when my marriage broke up. I was devastated and felt guilty beyond description. I had lost my self-respect and couldn't face my friends. In fact, I felt that I had no friends anymore and more or less broke off all relationships because I was afraid to find out who was still my friend and who wasn't. This is a common mistake many newly divorced people make. I felt that I had lost everything I had worked for all of my life. We had a beautiful waterfront home in Tiburon overlooking the Golden Gate Bridge, had enjoyed a happy family life for twenty-one years, had many friends and I had had a successful business career.

*Square Peg - Round Hole Syndrome*

I had built two sales organizations from scratch and in both cases became the top region in the company. Then a business friend asked me if I would like to head up a new company that was being formed, which, if it were successful, would make me an unbelievable amount of money in the next two to five years. I accepted, disregarding that small inner voice that cautioned me against this move. Due to a set of circumstances beyond our control - in particular a new IRS ruling - the company lasted only two years. During those two years as president I felt out of place, out of my element. I didn't have the confidence in this position that I had before in sales management.

Following the demise of that company, I was again

approached to become the president of another company. I accepted and again spent a year and a half in a position in which I felt extremely uncomfortable and ineffective because I was dealing from my weaknesses, not my strengths. I found myself operating in areas where I was weakest and delegating responsibilities to others in areas where I excelled.

Through these two experiences, however, I learned a good lesson...if you're doing something that's working for you, keep doing it! I've discovered that people so often make this mistake of switching from something that they have been successful in doing.

To give you a picture of my lifestyle after the breakup of my marriage, I was forced to sleep on the sofa in my office in a sleeping bag. I had no other place to stay and couldn't afford an apartment. I lived this way for an entire year.

## *A Night of Revealing "Flashbacks"*

One night while I was unsuccessfully trying to get to sleep because I was plagued with problems, I remembered something my friend Helen Boyle, who is a psychologist, told me years ago. She had said, "People don't necessarily get out of life what they want, but everyone gets what he or she EXPECTS!" It suddenly hit me that I was expecting bad things to happen. I was expecting friends to turn their backs on me. I was expecting to fail.

Then, I also remembered Helen's husband, John Boyle, and some things he had taught me in a seminar I had taken from him sixteen years earlier. In this seminar, now called Omega Seminar, he taught me how to structure goals. He said, "Decide what you want, but you don't have to know how you are going to get it." In other words, the way will be opened up after you set your goals and direct your thinking toward them. Faith can do wonderful things, for by it we can very often lift ourselves into a state of mind that automatically puts us in tune with the good we desire. In our inner world we need certain spiritual rules to follow, much as we need such things as traffic and legal rules in our material world. There is no other age in which so much has been learned about the relationship between our thinking and the conditions of our life. Physicians are discovering more each day about the connecting link of thought and its effect upon the external conditions of a person's body and life. I've come to believe that life is truly a journey and the living and learning can be a rich and rewarding experience.

These things began to spin around in my mind that night. I remembered that John Boyle gave me the courage years before to buy our waterfront home at a time when I thought it was beyond our means. When I told him how much we wanted it, he said without hesitation, "Buy it!" Had it not been for him we would never have bought that home which proved to be a great delight to us for those sixteen years. I also began to recollect the affirmations he had taught me and how they had changed my life back then. I realized then that for no apparent reason I had stopped using them in recent years.

*Intuition Prompted Important Phone Calls*

That sleepless night five years ago in my office I picked up the telephone and called John Boyle and brought him up to date on what was happening in my life. I'll never forget his words that night. He said, "John, you are born to succeed! No matter what has happened, you'll be back on top!" With his inspiration, I told myself that I would be back on top! I knew that if positive goal-setting worked before, it would work again.

I stayed up most of that night deciding just where I wanted to go from there. I wrote down my goals and affirmations again for the first time in years. An idea popped into my head. I was excited because I knew that some powerful force outside myself was guiding my thoughts at that moment. I remembered how I had conducted special classes in the past for all of the salespeople who had worked for me - classes on how to set and attain goals. The memory of one specific person, John Gore of Sacramento, came into focus. He used those affirmations to become one of the most successful financial planners in his area. He told me and others how I had turned his life around, how I had taught him things he had never been exposed to before.

I also remembered Gerhard H. Stehr who came to see me when he was a student at UCLA. I remembered him saying that he wanted a part-time job selling mutual funds so that he could work his way through college. At the time, I could hardly understand him because he spoke such broken English, having just recently come here from Germany without speaking a word of English. However, I recognized that he had that special something inside of him that made him believe in himself. I hired him on a part-time basis and taught him what I had learned about setting high goals without worrying about how he was going to attain them. He used affirmations to program himself to expect to reach those goals. I remembered how, after he had graduated, he came to work full-time and set a goal to write a million dollars worth of mutual funds in one year. That was back in 1968, when a million dollars worth of mutual funds in one year was an impressive amount-but he did it! And, I remembered that he used to tell people how I had believed in him and had given him the start and inspiration he needed to be successful. Today he is one of the most successful financial planners in Southern California.

That night I remembered the satisfaction I had gotten out of teaching people how to be more effective and then watching the ones who used those techniques succeed far beyond their previous hopes or dreams.

Another person came to mind that night of "flash-backs" - Walfred Dick, who was a part-time mutual fund salesperson in Sacramento for a company when I was national sales manager. He attended an annual sales meeting where I gave a talk entitled, "What Makes A Pro?" Somehow he was at the right place at the right time and heard the right words. He said that my talk had inspired him to become the top producer in the firm and stay there year after year. He gave me credit both privately and publicly for saying those things that turned his career around.

I honestly believe that these memories began to stream through my mind that night to re-inspire me to do the same thing for myself. I began to see clearly that if these principles had worked for me before and had helped others I had taught in the past, that they would work for me again. I sat up suddenly and said, "Why are you lying here feeling sorry for yourself?" A miracle seemed to be happening as I saw the morning sunlight begin to peek through my office windows. That night my attitude had changed from "my life is over" to "I'm beginning a whole new life!" I told myself that I couldn't change the past and feeling guilty wouldn't undo any of the harm that had been done. I knew I possessed every winning quality that I had before - so, from that point on, things started to happen. Every seminar I conducted gave me more confidence and more clients. I moved into an apartment and recontacted friends I had not seen in a long time.

## My Career Blossomed Again

It has been over five years since that bleak period in my life and I can now state that I have achieved many of my goals, one of which was to become financially independent and successful once again in a career. I have personally interviewed and counselled over 2,500 people in Marin County and helped them to successfully invest over $15 million dollars. One of the things I discovered,

incidentally, through my interviews with these people was
that the mere possession of sizable sums of money did not
necessarily constitute "wealth". Many of those who had
thousands of dollars to invest were actually almost
destitute emotionally, and lacked "peace of mind" which
Napoleon Hill called the "wealth" without which we have
no wealth.

This year I was asked to conduct three workshops at
the National Convention of the International Association
of Financial Planners, which was held in Boston. My
subject was "How To Promote and Conduct Financial
Planning Seminars". Eleven hundred people from all over
the country attended these workshops. One of the most
interesting things to me was the reaction of one of my
friends before I flew East. He asked me why I was going
there to teach my competitors how to conduct seminars
like those I had been successfully conducting. I feel he
missed the point completely. I know, without a doubt,
that by giving to other people we receive far more in
return - maybe not from that person or group, but in
many unexpected ways.

Another person, Joe Leadem, came to see me a little
over a year ago feeling very depressed. Although he had
been in the mutual fund industry for many years as a
wholesaler, he decided to start a private financial
planning practice. Things were not going well with him
and he wanted to know the specifics of what I was doing.
So, I shared with Joe everything that I had learned from
my experience in the past five years conducting financial
planning seminars. I gave him all of the facts he would
need to start doing the same thing in his area. Today he is
extremely successful, earning more money than he had
ever earned in his life. Money cannot buy the feeling of
satisfaction that one gets from participating in experiences like that when you have been a positive factor in
someone's life.

*High Expectations Have Been Fulfilled*

Not only has my business life been restored, but about four and one-half years ago I met an attractive woman who has made it possible for me to know more joy, contentment and real love than I thought existed. We were married about a year and a half ago and today have a very rewarding relationship that allows us to share our individual lives without smothering each other. I have experienced a tremendous feeling of peace and harmony and feel completely at ease in her company, and she has expressed the same reaction. We found each other at just the right time in our lives. We have a lovely home in Mill Valley, a large circle of friends all of whom have commented that we seem to "bring out the best in each other and are good for each other." I expected to find the right person, and did! I expected to be successful in my career again, and am!

*Gratitude To Four Other "Power-Packed" People*

I would like to give credit to four other people who have been very helpful to me far beyond the call of duty in a very power-packed way. Back in 1971, I was in Phoenix on business. At that time, I had ambitions of becoming a professional speaker, although I had no specific plans for how or when I would start doing it. However, it was one of my goals at the time and is again today. I called Cavett Robert, whom I had heard speak a number of times, and feel is one of the most inspiring speakers on the circuit. I told him of my ambition and that I would like to meet him sometime. He graciously invited my wife and me to dinner, along with Merlyn Cundiff, another professional speaker who had achieved success. He and Merlyn spent the entire evening openly sharing their experiences and how they had gotten started. This was long before the

National Speakers Association had been organized, incidentally. It was amazing to me at the time that this well-known man who didn't even know me was willing to spend his entire evening to help me get started by sharing his knowledge. Because other responsibilities and directions were present in my life at the time, I didn't do anything about it then, but still remember his positive advice today.

Bill Gove, whom I had also admired and respected as a speaker and a person for years, was equally as generous with his time and advice. I can remember him saying that when you give a speech to imagine that you are sitting in someone's living room talking to friends and to keep it friendly and conversational.

Now I have had some experience speaking and am directing myself toward a career as a professional speaker. I have developed an informal style, in keeping with Bill Gove's advice and find that it is right for me.

Another nationally-known speaker, Christopher Hegarty, has been spending time with me, offering me his help by avoiding some of the pitfalls and mistakes he made in the beginning years. All of these four have made an impact upon me and are helping me to develop my speaking skills.

I've also been discovering recently that the National Speakers Association, of which I am a member, is full of other sharing, positive power people who give freely of themselves to help newcomers.

My present goal is to grow as a speaker and be able to inspire those who hear me to be positive in the pursuit of their goals and to, perhaps, touch their lives at just that magic moment. I truly believe that a higher power works in exciting ways to use each of us in sustaining each other at critical points in our journey and that we are meant to lead power-packed lives.

*"There is always room for persons of force, and they make room for many."*

Emerson

The Enlightenment Amplifiers

**ELIZABETH AND HAYS BARHYDT**
Loving Life
8005 Bleriot Avenue
Los Angeles, California 90045
(213) 641-0567

## ELIZABETH BARHYDT

Elizabeth Barhydt was born in Philadelphia in the depths of depression, 1932. At age 4 the family moved again to a larger farm. Her schooling was interrupted at the 8th grade by scarlet fever and by her father's decision to keep the entire family working on the farm.

Elizabeth had very little experience of the outside world until she ran away from the farm at age 20. She spent most of her adult life in California where several of her brothers and sisters live. She worked mostly as a bookkeeper and clerk, learning the trade on the job.

After repeated failures in finding the love and happiness she craved, Elizabeth in 1979 at age 45 discovered Ken Keyes, Jr., author of "HANDBOOK TO HIGHER CONSCIOUSNESS", participating in a week long training at his Berkeley Living Love Center. Several months later Elizabeth moved on to Cornucopia, Ken's new training center in St. Mary, Kentucky, and over a period of eleven months created a major transformation in her life through the daily practice and experience of Ken's Living Love methods.

Elizabeth met Hap Barhydt at Cornucopia and returned with him to Los Angeles to create a marriage based on Ken's book "CONSCIOUS PERSON'S GUIDE TO RELATIONSHIPS", to continue the mutual growth through continued study, principally at the Healing Light Center, and to share their experience with other people. Elizabeth and Hap have organized the Loving Life Church as a non-profit vehicle for conducting workshops and support group meetings for people interested in learning about and practicing the Living Love methods.

# THE POWER OF LOVING

*By Elizabeth Barhydt*

*"For now we see in a mirror dimly, but then face to face.
Now I know in part; then I shall understand fully, even as
I have been fully understood. Now faith, hope and love
remain, these three; the greatest of these is love."*
St. Paul, I Corinthians, 13:12-13

I made this promise to myself when I ran away from
home, "When my father dies, I will go to his funeral." I
wanted to make sure it was he they were burying six feet
under! That was a heartful of hate. Whenever anything
went wrong, I would continue to build my case of hate
against him.

If only I had a decent father...

If only I had been allowed to go to school...

If only I didn't stutter...

If only I wasn't sick...

I went on and on, proving my case. I was right! But

this anger did not make me happy. My head told me everything was O.K. in my new life, but in my guts it was "YUK". I had brought my misery with me.

## My Beautiful Dream

I was a daydreamer. I spent my childhood in my own little world of make believe, fantasies, and dreams. I dreamed about my Beautiful Happy World, and how someday I was going to escape and find it.

When I was fifteen years old, I wrote a letter to Roy Rogers asking him to come and rescue me from my unhappy life. I was very sad and lonely. I did not have any friends and did not expect to have any either. I lived on an isolated farm in Pennsylvania with my parents and brothers and sisters. I did not get along with any of them. In fact when anything at all went wrong, they always blamed me for it whether I did it or not, and I was always punished. When I tried to defend myself, the punishment was that much more severe. I tried to please Father in every way possible, but no matter what I did Father was never satisfied.

When I was twenty years old, I realized Roy Rogers was not going to rescue me. If I could find the Beautiful Happy World of my dreams, I was going to have to do it for myself. Until this time in my life, I had never talked on a telephone and had never crossed a street by myself. I stuttered terribly and was quite sick physically. Father said my being sick was just an attempt to get out of work. I knew if I did not leave this unhappy farm I would die and never find my Beautiful Happy World. So I planned my escape carefully.

## My Escape

Mother no longer lived on the farm but came to visit us

often. Each time when one of sisters took Mother to the bus station, I made sure I went along. I learned how Mother asked for the ticket, how much it cost, and where to get on the bus. I sneaked pennies, nickels, and dimes from Father's dresser for bus fare, just a little at a time; so I would not get caught. I smuggled a duffle bag from the attic and hid it under the floor boards of the abandoned chicken coop with my personal things, my precious Roy Rogers scrapbook, a faded dress, and the good clothes I was going to wear when I left. I carefully checked the duffle bag from time to time to make sure nobody had discovered it.

All was going well until one Sunday when Father decided we would all get dressed in our good clothes and go to the park for the afternoon, but my new clothes were in the old chicken coop. How was I going to get them back into the house without getting caught? Father saved me in spite of himself. He started drinking. The more he drank, the angrier he got. The trip to the park was cancelled.

Then there was another close call. Father decided to ask two of my brothers to clean out the chicken coop. I thought this time I would surely be discovered. But again something happened, and the chicken coop was momentarily forgotten.

Finally Father realized someone was taking money from his dresser. Now I knew I had to leave quickly. I told Father I was going to weed the potato patch by the chicken coop. By nine o'clock I was on my way wearing my good clothes, a new pair of jeans, a white shirt, and loafers. I left my dirty clothes in the potato patch, where they would be sure to be found, with a note saying, "This is the only way I can leave. I can't take the chance to ask."

I walked the four miles into town rapidly and went straight to the bus station. Because I stuttered, I pinned a note to my shirt saying I could not talk and with instructions on where I wanted to go.

## The Search

For many years I searched everywhere for my dream of my Beautiful Happy World. I hated my father so much that I wanted to prove him wrong, to show him that there was indeed a Beautiful Happy World out there.

I started my search in a nearby city, sewing labels in women's lingerie to earn my way. In time I crossed the country to California, still searching. After an unhappy love affair, I moved on to Hawaii, thinking my life there would be different. I worked as a bookkeeper in a bank, where everything on the application was a lie except for my name in order to get the job. Then as an Arthur Murray dance instructor, hoping the right person would come alone. And ultimately as a rate clerk for a trucking firm where I earned very good money, but found little satisfaction. A brief marriage spoiled a beautiful friendship and ended in divorce. Every job, every relationship was the same. Things were not any different than they were back on the farm in Pennsylvania. I still could not get along with people.

Father had said people are only good to you because they want something from you. There is no point in having friends if they will not take time to visit when you are sick or need help. People will use you for sex, but if you do not have sex you will go crazy. People are out to get you; they are no good.

Father was right. My dream was shattered. There was no Beautiful Happy World out there. I did not want to live anymore. By the time I was 45 I was ready to pull the plug on my life.

## The Solution

Then something happened, a miracle of sorts. My sister

asked me to go to a week long Living Love training by Ken Keyes, Jr., author of "HANDBOOK TO HIGHER CONSCIOUSNESS". My first reaction was, "No way!" I had already spent over $2,000 on analyst's fees. I felt I was doomed, and nobody could help me. I wanted to die, but for her sake I would go. That was what I told myself. But the real truth was I did not want people to know I was a closet drinker and took tranquilizers at the same time, a fatal combination.

Perhaps I did go to that workshop to keep my sister company, but by the time three days were up I knew that I was there for me and that there was a way I could find my Beautiful Happy World, using Ken Keyes' Living Love Way.

That week became one of the most fantastic weeks I had ever spent: singing awareness songs, lots of love and support, and much more. But I was still afraid, fearful, sad, lonely and frustrated. I was one of those people who put on a good front, but I was afraid someone might find out I was a phoney. Now I was ready to hear the message, to take responsibility for my feelings, and to stop blaming others.

In my head I could hear the words, but my inner guts were still tied up in knots. I thought maybe there might be something in this Living Love stuff; so before I actually pulled the plug on my life, I would give life one more try.

I left my job, rented out my house, gave away most of my things, packed what was left into the trunk of my automobile, and drove off to Cornucopia in St. Mary, Kentucky, Ken Keyes' new live-in training center.

There my life started to unfold, and my hate began turning to love. I saw how I had set myself up for my own unhappiness, how I chose to create suffering in any given situation, and that I alone had the power to take charge of my life. I no longer had to be a yo-yo running mindlessly up and down the jerking string of life.

*Unconditional Love*

Yes, I did go back home to my father's funeral. That happened eight years after my escape. My heart was indeed filled with hate as I returned to watch him being buried. But now I have opened my heart to a new view.

Father died of the not-so-rare disease known as a broken heart. When Father took sick, Mother, whom he had sent away many years earlier, came back to the farm to take care of him. Father had no love for Mother. He did not have anything good to say about her. He hated her with a passion, but Mother loved him in spite of it all and wanted to take care of him when he was sick. Father let Mother stay for a while, but more and more he stayed in bed.

One day my sister asked Father why he did not get out of bed like he used to. "Not until she leaves", he said, referring to my mother. My sister asked, "If Mother left, would you get out of bed?" He said he would. Mother did not leave, but my sister told Father that she had. Of course Father did not believe her. My sister replied, "If you don't believe me, then get up and look for yourself." He got out of bed and searched all the rooms downstairs. He went upstairs and searched all the rooms there. He looked in the basement, then went outside to check all around the house. He could not find her anywhere. He could not believe she had really gone. Then he went back to bed. With tears in his eyes he sobbed to my sister, "She really did leave!"

These were the last words Father spoke. He went into a coma, and two days later he was dead. Father was pleading to the last. His eyes told the story, "Love me the way I am; I tried."

Mother did love him just the way he was, but that was not enough for Father. Father did not know how to receive the love he craved. He could not understand how Mother could love him after what he had done. He could not love himself or accept himself the way he was. He did not think he was worthy of Mother's love. Because having her there was so painful he sent her away, but in his heart he did not want her to go.

I ask myself, "Am I any different than my father?" Three years ago when I was drinking, taking tranquilizers, and ready to end my life, I too cried, "Won't someone please love me just the way I am?" I too did not know how to receive love. I could not love myself just the way I was; so I was unable to let anyone else love me. Many times I sent people out of my life because I did not think I was worthy of their love.

Loving is simply accepting another, and oneself, completely and unconditionally, just as we are. I may not agree that what Father did was right or may not like what he did, but on the emotional level I can accept and forgive him.

Now I know the power of my love will see me through. As long as I can love myself, which is not always easy to do, I can create happiness in my life. I am not dependent on what others say or do. Only when I am not loving myself do I want others to change. I am learning to love and accept myself right where I am, all the time.

My search is finally over. I have found my Beautiful Happy World. I had been looking in all the wrong places. It was inside of me all the time. Now that I am learning to be loving, my life is becoming beautiful and my dreams are coming true.

## Taking Charge

This new repsonsibility and power was difficult to take. It was hard for me to love and accept myself. However in time, through the love and support of the people at Cornucopia I learned that there was no way I had to be to love, or be loved, and that I could become free of robot-like emotional patterns. They taught me, "I am beautiful, lovable, and capable just as I am."

After lots of reprogramming, lots of tears, and lots of loving support, I started to see how Father loved me in the only way he knew how. My father was not any different than I am. Behind all our differences, on the emotional level we are ONE.

There is no right or wrong in life. I did not have to like what had happened in my life. I learned not to create suffering over things I cannot change. Father was doing only what he needed to do at that moment in his life. He was protecting me from the cruel outside world, as he saw it. What he did was a reflection of his opinions and his view of life. I had my own choices open to me.

*Opening the Door*

Learning to love opened the door of life. I met my husband, Hap, at Cornucopia and created a Living Love marriage, based on Ken Keyes' book, "A CONSCIOUS PERSON'S GUIDE TO RELATIONSHIPS." Hap gave me even more opportunities to learn and to expand my power to love. The Living Love relationship really works, when I do.

Upon completing our training at Cornucopia, Hap and I chose to return to California to continue our growth together and to share our experience with other people. We have organized the Loving Life Church in Los Angeles and are conducting workshops and support meetings for people interested in learning about and practicing the Living Love Methods.

Life is worth living. I keep reading the "HANDBOOK TO HIGHER CONSCIOUSNESS", my "bible", over and over again, because I continue to hear it at deeper and deeper levels. I use Ken Keyes' Living Love Methods at every moment when I feel negative, separating emotions. I sing the Living Love songs to myself to build my loving energy. These are now all part of my life, and I hold them in deeper levels of my consciousness. Whenever I need them they are there.

Whenever I am feeling low, I just tune into the Living Love Way and start to work accepting myself, right where I am. I accept myself when I am low, and I accept myself when I am high. Because it is all one; there is no difference. I like to share the Living Love Way with other people because I believe in its power. It works for me, and it can work for you. Acceptance is on the emotional level only; I can still work for people or situations to change.

*"Always bear in mind that your own resolution to succeed is more important than any other one thing."*
            *Abraham Lincoln*

*"Be tolerant among the intolerant, gentle among the violent, and free from greed among the greedy."*
*Buddha*

The Enlightenment Amplifiers

HELEN ANTONIAK, Ph.D.
1528 Monitor Rd.
San Diego, California 92110
(714) 287-6020    (714) 276-6858

## HELEN ANTONIAK

Helen Antoniak organized the San Diego Widowed to Widowed Program. She is co-author of ALONE: Emotional Legal and Financial Help for the Widowed or Divorced Woman. In cooperation with Ann Bennett Sturgis, Ph.D. of the Stress Management Training Institute, she designed a series of cassettes for people adjusting to the end of a marriage. The "Creative Widowhood Adjustment" cassettes and the "Creative Divorce Adjustment" cassettes are used all over the United States.

Even though Helen is an author, speaker, college teacher and real estate agent, she primarily identifies herself as a Social Worker. She obtained her Masters Degree in Social Work from San Diego State University in 1972. She is a member of the Academy of Certified Social Workers and the National Speakers Association. Recently she completed work toward a Ph.D. in Psychology. Helen's special areas of interest are grief adjustment, stress reduction and goal setting.

**22**

POSITIVE

POWER

PEOPLE

*The Enlightenment Amplifiers*

# THE POWER OF HELPING OTHERS THROUGH GRIEF

*By Helen Antoniak, Ph.D.*

*"The fatherless and the widow he sustains."*
*Psalm 146:9*

When I see someone who is nineteen, I always marvel at how young they are. I know when I was nineteen, I was convinced I was fully grown up and mature in every day. Then an event occurred in my life which propelled me into adulthood.

*Explosion-like Velocity*

I learned such a painful lesson that I have dedicated my life to easing that same pain for others. What seemed like a useless waste became the first step on a very positive path and a path that I can now look back upon and realize that I was guided all along the way.

It was the dawn of Saturday, June 3, 1967. It was the beginning of June Week at the United States Naval Academy and I was there! For me it was the culmination of a dream I had cherished in my heart long before my brother, Peter, was accepted as a Plebe four years before. The only way I could have been prouder was if I were graduating myself! (This was long before anyone even dared whisper the *possibility of female midshipmen*.

Annapolis! The name was magic for me. My father graduated from Annapolis, so right from the start I knew I was associated with the Navy. Even today I can tell you where my Dad placed his officer's hat as he came home when I was just a small child. When I was five and my mother gave me a "Navel orange" to eat, I wondered what fruit children whose fathers were in the Army got for snacks.

The Navy was a part of my life and the Naval Academy at Annapolis, Maryland was the heart of its rich tradition. When a television program called "Men of Annapolis" was on, I could be found faithfully perched in front of the set. I poured over a photographic essay book called "The Life of a Midshipman" until I almost had it memorized.

Finally I was there! My father and mother and I had driven all the way across the United States from San Diego. The trip had proven relatively uneventful. Since my brother would be on leave after the graduation ceremonies, the trip would then continue with the four of us traveling up to the World's Fair in Canada.

The journey had been a little pushed since we had waited until I finished my final exams at the University of San Diego.

Just finding lodging in Annapolis for June Week is a major feat. My brother rented for us a little cottage which was in front of a large family home near the water. Somehow, in the course of getting the key and unloading the car, I discovered that our landlord was a doctor.

Sleep that night came easy. The cottage was stuffy from having been closed up, and the windows were painted shut, but I was too tired to worry about any of that. The next morning I was awakened by a peculiar sound. My father had already gotten up and showered. He was breathing very loudly. My initial reaction was annoyance but it quickly changed to concern. Dad was back on top of his bed in the little bedroom. I dressed quickly. Even though I had never been confronted by a situation like this before, I knew it was urgent that Mom and I get help.

I ran frantically to the front door of the doctor. It seemed forever before he answered, and forever again before he dressed and came to our cottage. It probably was only a matter of minutes but I knew my dad needed help and he needed it fast.

Soon we were all in the bedroom. The doctor kept asking loudly, "Sir, are you in pain?" Shortly before I had heard dad tell mom to pray when she asked what she could do for him, but now he was not responding.

We all sprang into action. While my mom went to call an ambulance, the doctor pounded my father's chest, as I did mouth-to-mouth resuscitation. Periodically the doctor would stop and feel my dad's pulse.

Finally the ambulance arrived and the paramedics joined our frantic efforts. First there was the plastic device that they pulled out of its wrapping, and pushed down my father's throat. Then they brought in a breathing apparatus. It was quite an effort to get my dad out of the tiny bedroom, the bed had collapsed from all of us administering our lifesaving efforts.

Dad had played on the football team at the Academy and although he was fifty-five, he still had the husky build associated with football players. Somehow, we finally had him on a stretcher in the living room. I remember focusing on his strong, stocky arm and broad hand, hanging limply off the side of the stretcher. "He is unconscious", I told myself.

I always wonder why they let me ride in the ambulance. Mom would have been the logical choice. Usually they don't take anybody, but somehow I was seated and we were speeding down the streets toward the Naval Academy infirmary. The paramedics labored over my dad as I bravely uttered reassurances. "We are almost there", I assured him.

I followed the stretcher right into the emergency room. First one person and then another asked me to leave. Somehow in the back of my mind I knew Jackie Kennedy had stayed by President Kennedy right into the operating theater. I was trying not to believe that things were as serious as they were. One of the corpsmen said to another, "Why are you giving him oxygen? He is not breathing." My mind was telling me how dangerous it is for the brain to be without oxygen for an extended period of time.

What sort of bargains do you make with God at a time like that? Of course, you want him alive and healthy. What about a compromise? How about alive and brain damaged? How about crippled for life and in a convalescent hospital? Dad was so intelligent and vigorous he could never stand to be an invalid, even if I was willing to bargain for his life at the cost of its quality.

But there were no "deals" that morning in the little waiting area of the emergency room. Even before mom arrived I knew it was all over. The chaplain was summoned and we were brought into an office. Soon some tranquilizers were ordered for Mom. My brother ran in already red-eyed from crying.


*He Was Gone*

It was my first close encounter with death. Both my grandmothers had died when I was in my teens, but they were old and ill. The overwhelming impact was not the same. This was different. This was my father dying before my eyes. One minute he was the man who had just driven us all the way across the country, the next minute he was gone forever.

Even though I know a lot more about life and death now, that final reality still amazes me. How can a person be alive one minute and dead the next? I was only nineteen, I knew very little about death, and virtually nothing about the intense pain that the entire family would soon be experiencing.

I now realize what the word "grief" meant. I suppose that somewhere in my mind I knew that my father would not live forever, especially in light of previous episodes related to his heart. No intellectual information could have prepared me for the emotional impact of the grief experience. It was like the difference between reading the word "lightning" and have a bolt shatter the air above your head.

The first thing that is striking about people who experience a severe emotional blow is how little the storm that is going on inside is reflected on the outside. My brother was still due to graduate and would have to remain at the Naval Academy regardless of our family loss. The chaplain recommended that my mother and I remain for the graduation ceremonies and this seemed like the best course of action. Shedding many tears, we went through the motions of families participating in "June Week".

It was an entire week after my father's death before we were back in San Diego attending his funeral. The time and miles, as well as the suddenness of his death, compounded the unreality of the situation.

The impact of our loss reverberated through our lives in a thousand different ways in the year that followed. At each corner was a new tunnel of emptiness and longing. Since we flew back, the car arrived several weeks after we did, having been driven across the country by a "drive away" service. Many of my father's clothes and personal effects, packed for what was to be a happy trip, were now sadly removed from the trunk. My parents 33rd wedding anniversary was June 15th.

Special family events, such as birthdays, would come and go. Big events like Thanksgiving and Christmas would never be the same. There was an incredible vacuum caused by Dad's absence. There was a hollow feeling inside of me.

People who have not experienced a family loss may have the illusion that families fall on each other's shoulders in warm support like something you might see on "The Waltons." This isn't how it was for us and not for most of the people I have talked with since that time.

## We Missed Him

Each member of the family was missing a different person, since all relationships are unique. My brother, Peter, was upset that he hadn't immediately told dad about the special award for his solar energy research he was receiving at the graduation ceremony. Peter was sure we hadn't done enough to save Dad's life. Mom felt she should not have permitted Dad to drive, and probably we could have saved his life if only she had accepted a neighbor's offer of an oxygen cannister before we left. My older brother, Charles, and his wife felt things were terribly unfair. My sister, Mary Ellen, the oldest in the family, was not only married but had three children with a fourth on the way. She lived in Monterey Park, which was over one-hundred miles away. She wanted to help, yet was already missing our father very much, and had all the demands of a young family.

There were not any family feuds or fights over inheritances. It was just that we each suffered in our own way and were ill-equipped to offer solace to each other or to mom, who certainly was experiencing the most intense loss.

That summer, there were three major activities in which I involved myself. One was a Spanish class which was necessary to complete a language requirement before my transfer from the University of San Diego to U.C.L.A. The second was a part-time job at a day care center, the third was picking up on certain projects my father had begun around the house.

I undertook gardening projects, painting projects, and even carpentry projects, which entailed the use of a huge, noisy table saw. Looking back on these efforts, I am reminded of a song from a musical presentation of Little Women. "I'm the man of the house now that Papa is away." I really had done none of this handywork before, but I threw myself into the activity as though my very future depended on completion of my Dad's plans.

In the fall, I began attending U.C.L.A. It was a difficult thing to do. I was following through on a decision I had made with both mom and dad's consent. Dad's death didn't change anything, yet it changed everything! I can still remember writing down my father's address, as the "Holy Cross Cemetery", on one of many forms required by UCLA!

I was fortunate that both Social Security and the Veteran's Administration sent me monthly checks for my two years at U.C.L.A. I lived in one of the dormitories and did my best to absorb myself into life at the big university. It was extremely difficult for me to leave mother all alone. (Peter was already engaged in naval training before being sent off to Viet Nam.)

There is a natural irritability families can get caught up in as each member grieves over his or her own loss. Even though I knew I wanted to continue my education at U.C.L.A., I felt I was abandoning mother by leaving her alone. I don't remember ever consciously thinking it at the time, but I am sure that subconsciously I feared that she too might suddenly die.

Any man that slightly resembled my father could instantly be the victim of a heart attack in my anxious imaginings. When my brother was doing his tour of duty in Viet Nam, I was expecting momentarily to receive word of his death. (He survived two tours of duty there with nothing more than a case of mumps.)

*It is Alright to Grieve*

When I arrived at U.C.L.A., I bore the hidden wounds of the recently bereaved. I knew I felt terrible, and I knew it had some relationship to my father's death, but I was totally unable to articulate what was going on inside me. I even made a feeble effort at getting help from the University Counseling Center by participating in a group. Still, I could never bring myself to tell them what was really bothering me. I needed somebody to say *it was alright to grieve* for the father you dearly loved, and who had died in front of you just months before, however the counselors were very poor at mindreading. It was months even before I could tell my roommate, who eventually became my best friend, that I had lost my father.

Looking back now, I can see how wrong it was to keep such pain within. I was harboring a deep dark secret. That is the interesting thing about how our emotions differ from our intellect. We can do dumb things from an intellectual viewpoint when we are overwhelmed by emotions. It would be several years before I would be able, for the first time, to put an *intellectual* light on that *emotional* experience. In the meanwhile, Mom and the rest of us muddled our way through the months which finally became the first year and then the second.

After graduation from U.C.L.A., I spent the next six months discovering for myself what everyone had been saying. "There is not a great market out there for someone with a Bachelors in Social Welfare." I returned home, held down a few odd jobs and eventually put in my application to begin work on a Masters degree in Social Work.

I suppose it was one of those red-letter days when I was accepted into the School of Social Work at San Diego State University, but the turning point in my life came several months later. Fortunately social work is one of those fields of endeavor where you can actually get out and do something while you are pondering over the academic part. We had several days a week of what was called "field placement." This was an opportunity to actually get out and practice the skills we were studying. There were many different social service agencies which students were assigned to. I was given a senior citizens center. There, I participated in a "Cheer Visitation" training course given by a social worker who had graduated a few years ahead of my class and was working full time in the field of geriatrics.

## Natural Grief Process

This is when enlightenment suddenly dawned. I was there to make the room look full, my thoughts fading in and out of my day-dreaming when the instructor began talking about the *natural grief process*. Suddenly I was all ears. So that's what I was experiencing! That's what Mom was experiencing! Why, the whole family had gone through it and NOBODY EVER TOLD US IT WAS NORMAL! That tiny bit of information given as one point in a series, was an incredible revelation to me.

A burden was lifted off my shoulders. I had been given a vision that was clear, almost of a celestial nature. It was suddenly obvious to me that widows needed a place to go where they could be told they were going through a normal grief process. I pictured an office with a desk, I saw a widow sitting next to the desk, being told by the interviewer that she was experiencing something NORMAL. It was a NORMAL GRIEF PROCESS.

I couldn't get over the simplicity of the whole thing. I knew right then and there that things would have been a whole lot easier for Mother and our family if we just had been told the simple secret of normal grief!

It was a full two years before my vision of a widow being counseled about her normal grief process was to become a reality. I am not sure when I realized that *I was to be the counselor* sharing that important secret.

I was just a few months into my two-year graduate program which would result in a Masters degree in Social Work. My special vision didn't get me out of even one hour of any class I had to attend. There wasn't even time in my personal schedule to pursue the dream on my own. I talked about it to anyone who I thought would understand, but my first real step was to undertake a research paper on services available to widows in San Diego County. There were none specifically for them, although they could get help for other problems.

In researching the library archieves, I discovered the name of a sociology professor who had written several articles on widowhood. I sent a letter off to the University of Washington where he taught. A month later, I received a reply from Florida. I had asked him, "Was there any program anywhere to help bereaved people?" Much to my delight, the answer was in the affirmative. There is such a program in Boston, Massachusetts, it is called 'Widow to Widow''. He gave the address; he also sent me a thick bibliography of books and articles related to death and dying.

This was another big day in my life! My letter to Boston not only brought me detailed information about a grief program, but the names of two women in San Diego who were also interested in a program for widows.

## Step by Step

All this took place a decade ago, but I still remember it vividly. Looking back, I see just how marvelously things fell into place, step by step. When I was young, I used to wish that God would send an angel that would appear to me in my bedroom one night and very clearly spell out what I was to do with my life. This has never happened, yet so many times when things seem impossible, they suddenly all work out. In the course of my development of the San Diego Widowed to Widowed Program, there were dozens and dozens of times when some seeming coincidence turned out to be just the missing link in piecing together the puzzle.

My fleeting vision of an office where a widow could come and understand that what she was going through was normal, started me on a ten-year adventure. Eventually, I was not just to have *one* office, but a *beautiful office suite*. Not only widows, but widowers as well, came to hear the reassuring message. The Widowed to Widowed Program became incorporated and provided much more than just individual counseling. We had group meetings, a twenty-four hour hotline, community education, a newsletter and a wide variety of special events. Eventually, I wrote a book with two other women which spread our message to an even wider audience than the thousands who over the years came to participate in our program. (The book was published in 1979 by Celestial Arts Press, it is called Alone, Emotional, Legal and Financial Help for the Widowed or Divorced Woman.) With the help of Dr. Ann Sturgis, Director of the Stress Management Training Institute, I designed and produced a series of stress reduction cassettes for daily use by newly bereaved people. (Creative Widowhood Adjustment Cassettes, Stress Management Training Institute, 2240 Caminito Precioso Sur, La Jolla, California 92037).

Both the book and the cassette series center around a formula which developed in my mind over the years of my work with widowed persons. Although the same topics and concerns were covered again and again, I had never had a reason to systemize them until my best friend's father died of a heart attack. I wanted to do something to make things easier for her and her mother. I wrote my advice to her, since she lived hundreds of miles away. The guidelines eventually became what I call the "One Year Recovery Guarantee". It is a set of positive suggestions that I have found virtually guarantees recovery from the normal problems of widowhood, if the person conscientiously applies them.

Here is our Recovery Guarantee. We hope this formula can help you, or someone you love.

### THE WIDOWED TO WIDOWED ONE-YEAR RECOVERY GUARANTEE

The Widowed to Widowed Program hereby guarantees almost complete recovery from the normal problems of grief and widowhood within one year if the participant complies with the following stipulations.

### *FINANCIAL AND LEGAL WELL BEING*

*1. Keep careful records of all your transactions. Photo copy all forms before sending them off and note where and when you sent them. Keep all documents received as well as carbons of your replies.*
*2. Maintain a written log of all the people you talk to on the phone concerning business, legal and financial matters [the bank, social security, mortuary, your lawyer]. Include in your log a summary of your questions and their answers.*
*3. Set up a bookkeeping system that you can live with.*

*Include in this some budget calculations concerning your regular expenses.*

*MENTAL WELL BEING*

*4. At least once, carefully read the booklet "On Being Alone." [This booklet is available through the American Association of Retired Persons [AARP]. Contact your local chapter for a copy or write Widowed Person Service, 1909 K Street, Washington, D.C. 20049].*

*5. Read at least five books related to widowhood and grief so that you are knowledgeable about the normal course of this life event.*

*PHYSICAL WELL BEING*

*6. Establish or maintain habits conducive to good health. These should include regular well-balanced meals, drinking plenty of water, getting regular moderate exercise and following a satisfactory sleep pattern.*

*7. Learn and use at least one relaxation technique that works for you. This may be self hypnosis, biofeedback, transcendental meditation, yoga or something else acceptable to you.*

*8. Avoid excesses in any habits. Do not drink more coffee or alcohol, eat more sweets or suddenly go on a crash diet, smoke more cigarettes, or do anything else more than you did before your loss. This applies to extreme busyness or extreme inactivity as well.*

*PSYCHOLOGICAL WELL BEING*

*9. Keep a written journal or tapes of your experiences and feelings during this year. Include recollections of dreams, random thoughts and letters you will never send.*

*10.Maintain or cultivate a close friendship with at least one person whom you are able to call at two o'clock in the morning because you need to talk and who will listen without criticism.*

*11.Work on an album, scrapbook or some other project which will help you crystalize and preserve the memories of your spouse for yourself and children, grandchildren and friends. While you savor these memories, realize that life is going on and you are closing the door on the past to open new doors.*

12. *Listen politely to friends, relatives, and neighbors giving advice. Note all the pressures that are being made on you but resolve to make no major decisions unless they are absolutely necessary.*

13. *Continue or find at least one pleasurable treat in your life which you can enjoy at least weekly. This could be a hobby, sport, club or organization, going out to lunch, or taking a special trip as long as it is something that you truly enjoy and that you will be able to treat yourself to regularly. This is a difficult time and you deserve to pamper yourself.*

14. *Treat unsolicited advice and pressures from others as water off a duck's back. You may listen politely and attentively but resolve not to make any major decision within this year unless absolutely necessary. Be especially wary of business ventures with friends or relatives.*

15. *Give yourself permission to cry. Do not give yourself negative messages such as "not here in front of these people..." or "I am only feeling sorry for myself." Let the tears flow. There is nothing more therapeutic than a "good cry."*

16. *If you become concerned about your state of mind, you think you are "going crazy," or you find yourself contemplating suicide, seek professional help immediately. Don't stop until you find a counselor you feel comfortable with. Keep working with your counselor, be he or she a psychiatrist, psychologist, social worker, pastor or whomever, until you have worked through your problems and set new goals. People who use professional help when they need it are smarter and saner than those who don't!*

*SOCIAL WELL BEING*

17. *Participate in at least seven activities of the Widowed to Widowed Program.*

18. *Read at least one book on assertiveness and preferably enroll in a course in assertiveness training. Be honest with your friends, neighbors, relatives, and fellow employees. If you are going through a particularly difficult time, let them know. If they are doing - or not doing - something and it is upsetting you [such as not talking about your spouse], let them know what you would prefer. If you really want to be left alone or included in something, let them know. You cannot expect people to be mindreaders. Even though your need may seem very obvious to you, give people the benefit of the doubt by spelling it out to them. Remember! Communication is not easy even in the best of times.*

*PHILOSOPHICAL WELL BEING*

19. *If you are a member of a church or religious group, spend some time learning more about their philosophy concerning the final stage of our life cycle, death. If you are not a member of such a group and do not find one you can comfortably fit into, spend time fitting the reality of death into your own philosophy of life.*

*"Youth when lightened and alive and given a sporting chance is strong for struggle and not afraid of any toils or punishments or dangers or deaths."*
*Carl Sandburg*